BLAZING THE WILDERNESS ROAD WITH DANIEL BOONE IN AMERICAN HISTORY

Other titles *in American History*

IN
AMERICAN
HISTORY

BLAZING THE WILDERNESS ROAD WITH DANIEL BOONE IN AMERICAN HISTORY

Carl R. Green

Enslow Publishers, Inc.

40 Industrial Road   PO Box 38
Box 398   Aldershot
Berkeley Heights, NJ 07922 Hants GU12 6BP
USA   UK

http://www.enslow.com

This book is dedicated to my granddaughters,
Evangeline & Valerie Green—spirited pioneers
in a new millennium.

Library of Congress Cataloging-in-Publication Data

Green, Carl, R.
   Blazing the Wilderness Road with Daniel Boone in American history /
Carl R. Green.
      p. cm. — (In American history)
   Includes bibliographical references (p. 118) and index.
   Summary: Discusses the Wilderness Road, a trail providing a route
from Tennessee to Kentucky in the late eighteenth and early nineteenth
centuries, Daniel Boone's role in its development, and life on the trail.
   ISBN 0-7660-1346-4
   1. Wilderness Road—Juvenile literature. 2. Boone, Daniel,
1734–1820—Juvenile literature. 3. Frontier and pioneer life—Tennessee,
East—Juvenile literature. 4. Frontier and pioneer life—Kentucky—Juvenile
literature. 5. Frontier and pioneer life—Virginia—Juvenile literature.
6. Tennessee, East—Description and travel—Juvenile literature.
7. Kentucky—Description and travel—Juvenile literature. 8. Virginia—
Description and travel—Juvenile literature. [1. Wilderness Road.
2. Frontier and pioneer life. 3. Boone, Daniel, 1734–1820.]
   I. Title. II. Series.

F454.G74 2000
976.9'02—dc21   99-462218

Printed in the United States of America

10 9 8 7 6 5 4 3 2 1

To Our Readers: All Internet addresses in this book were active and appropriate
when we went to press. Any comments or suggestions can be sent by e-mail to
Comments@enslow.com or to the address on the back cover.

Illustration Credits: *Authentic Civil War Illustrations*, Dover Publications,
Inc., (1995), p. 110 (inset); Bell County Historical Society, Middlesboro,
Kentucky, p. 79; Carl R. Green, pp. 14; 16, 21, 30, 32, 43, 49, 50, 51,
56, 68, 72, 83, 90, 94, 98, 106, 110; Library of Congress, pp. 53, 59;
National Archives, p. 38; *The American West in the Nineteenth Century*,
Dover Publications, Inc. (1992), pp. 18, 24, 64, 74, 99; Tom N.
Shattuck, Wilderness Road Tours, pp. 10, 108; *Trades and Occupations:
A Pictorial Archive from Early Sources*, Dover Publications, Inc., (1990),
p. 84; Western History Department, Denver Public Library, p. 85.

Cover Illustrations: Carl R. Green; Library of Congress; National
Archives.

★ CONTENTS ★

THE LAND OF TOMORROW

The United States of America did not always stretch "from sea to shining sea." For well over a century, the immigrants who flocked to the New World were mostly content to colonize the Atlantic Coast. In time, explorers and hunters returned from journeys into the wilderness with tales of wondrous lands beyond the horizon. Colonists who felt the coastal plains were becoming too crowded began to dream of building new lives farther west.

After the Revolutionary War, a schoolteacher's book opened a new chapter in the story of the westward movement. John Filson had floated down the Ohio River and wandered through a far-off territory called Kentucky. When he returned he wrote about the land and its great hero in a book called *Adventures of Colonel Daniel Boone, One of the Original Settlers of Kentucke*. Readers were inspired by Filson's tales of this legendary explorer, hunter, soldier, and road-builder. Their eyes burned even brighter when they read about Kentucky.

This is a country, Filson wrote, that flows "with milk and honey, a land of brooks and water, . . . a land of wheat and barley, and all kinds of fruits. You shall eat bread without scarceness, and not lack any thing in it." The climate, he promised, was springlike, neither too hot nor too cold. "Thus," he concluded, "your country [is] favoured with the smiles of heaven."[1]

Kentucky fever swept the land, but those who hoped to move westward faced daunting hurdles. Kentucky-bound settlers had to find a way through a tangled wilderness and across a range of mountains. Some braved rapids, sandbars, and hostile American Indians as they floated down the Ohio River. A far greater number chose to follow a route that Boone had carved out in 1775. Known as the Wilderness Road, the trail bristled with dangers—but it led to a new life in Kentucky.

Historian A. B. Hulbert asks that we pay tribute to the Wilderness Road. "The footsteps of the tens of thousands who have passed over it," he writes, "have left a trace that a thousand years cannot eradicate. . . . For when all is said, this track from tidewater through Cumberland Gap must remain a monument to the courage and patriotism of the people of old Virginia and North Carolina."[2]

The Quest for "Elbow Room"

Long before the Wilderness Road became a reality, America's first colonists planted their crops and built their towns close to the Atlantic seaboard. Slowly at first, and then in greater numbers, the new settlers pushed westward. By the mid-1700s the edge of the frontier was nearing the Appalachian Mountains. Was there truly a vast and fertile wilderness beyond that rugged mountain range? Hunters and traders returned from their journeys to report that the Cherokee called the land *Ken-tah-teh*. Some said the name meant "meadowland." Others said it translated as "tomorrow," "the land where we will live."[3]

The lure of the new land increased as more people crowded into the coastal plains and inland valleys. Hunters complained that game was growing scarce. Planters saw their tobacco crops fail as the thin layer of topsoil lost fertility. Most of all, these new Americans wanted elbow room. The sight of smoke rising from nearby chimneys gave backcountry farmers the feeling that the world was crowding in on them. Wherever settlers gathered, someone was sure to talk about picking up and moving west. Most felt certain that the land many called *Kaintuckee* would fulfill their dreams. But first they had to find a passage across the mountains for their horses and wagons.

Thomas Walker Leads the Way

Dr. Thomas Walker could have lived a safe, quiet existence on his Virginia plantation. Instead, he waved good-bye to his family and led an expedition westward into the wilderness. Walker and his partners in the Loyal Land Company of Virginia owned the rights to survey and settle eight hundred thousand acres of western land. The rights were useless, however, until someone blazed a trail through the mountains. Once he reached Kentucky, Walker planned to lay claim to his share of that fabled meadowland.

Walker and his five companions turned their horses westward on March 6, 1750. Ahead lay the Appalachian Mountains, a rugged range that stretches south from Canada into central Alabama. Walker had heard tales of an easy route across the mountains, but none of the European settlers knew where to find it. He also hoped to disprove rumors that Kentucky was bitterly cold. A forest of huge trees, old stories warned, kept the sun's

In 1750, Dr. Thomas Walker rode west to find a route that would lead across the Appalachian Mountains and into the fabled land of Kentucky. A long, hard trek through rugged country led Walker and his companions to the pass they sought—the Cumberland Gap.

rays from reaching the ground. The maps of the day showed only a blank space between the mountains and the Mississippi River. The French claimed the land, but Virginians believed their claim was stronger. The Europeans did not give a second thought to the rights of the American Indian tribes whose trails crisscrossed the region.

Walker followed a route that led across the upland plateau known as the Piedmont Region. From there he crossed the Blue Ridge Mountains into the Great Valley of the Appalachians. Along the way the men stopped at small farms to rest for the night. The farmers welcomed the visitors and invited them into their snug log cabins. Walker saw that these backwoods folk were leaving Old World ways behind. Even the language was changing. Out here, fish that the English called perch and mullet were known as rocks and fatbacks. Springs that left deposits of salt behind had become licks, and river rapids were called riffles.[4]

For a time the men followed the Great Philadelphia Wagon Road. This well-traveled route wandered southward to the Yadkin River in North Carolina. At the Big Lick, where Roanoke, Virginia, would one day take root, Walker mourned the passing of the buffalo and elk. Too many hunters, he noted, were killing the animals for sport and leaving the bodies to rot. After leaving the lick Walker found his way to the middle fork of the Holston River. The last white man the party encountered was a German trader named Samuel

Stalnaker. When the men left after helping Stalnaker build a cabin, they plunged into a tangled wilderness.

At the end of each day's march the men cared for their horses, pitched a tent, and built a roaring fire. Hunters grabbed their flintlocks and prowled the woods, looking for game. A pair of fat pheasants or a venison steak made a welcome change from a diet of cornmeal and bacon. After dinner, Walker wrote in his journal and mended his elkskin moccasins. Later woodsmen would dress in deerskin, but Walker's party preferred woolen coats and soft-brimmed hats.[5]

A Long Trek Pays Off

As Walker led his party onward, the weather turned ugly. Lightning flashed, and a driving rain soaked through the men's coats. The cold crept into their bones as the horses threaded their way past giant poplars and twisted oaks. To raise spirits, Walker read aloud from the Bible each night as the men huddled in their tent.

One snowy morning the explorers found signs that American Indians had passed along a nearby creek. No one felt alarmed, for Virginia was at peace with the western tribes. A few days later the dogs flushed two buffalo calves from their hiding place. The men joined the chase as the frightened calves bucked and dodged. They cornered one calf, only to see it butt Walker in the stomach and break free. After a no-holds-barred wrestling match, the men threw and hog-tied both animals. That night they feasted on roast buffalo.

On April 9 the expedition forded the Clinch River near present-day Sneedville, Tennessee. The horses splashed across easily, but the men had to build a raft to float their baggage to the far shore. That night Walker wrote, "When the Raft was brought back, it was so heavy that it would not carry anything more dry. . . . We waded and carryed the remainder . . . on our shoulders at two turns over the River, which is about one hundred and thirty yards wide."[6] On another day Walker's dog came off second best in a scuffle with a bear. Walker dressed the deep gashes and carried the dog over his saddle while the wounds healed.

Four days later, on April 13, a high, dark ridge loomed ahead of the weary party. The men groaned at the thought of climbing one more mountain, but Walker pressed forward. Soon he came upon what he called a "plain Indian road." By sheer chance he had stumbled upon what American Indians called the Athawominee, or Warrior's Path. Later explorers would learn that the well-traveled path led north from the Carolinas as far as New York. To Walker's delight, the path soon led to a break in the mountain wall. He felt certain this was the path that would lead them into Kentucky.

As they climbed upward the men passed the entrance to a large cave. When he reached the summit, Walker promptly named the pass Cave Gap. On the trek down the far side, the path led through thick cane-brakes and tangled laurel groves. In one valley the men found a westward-flowing river, proof that they had

Whenever possible, Thomas Walker and his Virginians followed twisting trails cut by wandering herds of buffalo. Modern hikers trek through the same country on well-kept trails like those found in Cumberland Gap National Historic Park.

crossed into Kentucky. Walker called it the Cumberland River, in honor of a British general, the Duke of Cumberland. Later travelers picked up the name and applied it to the entire area. Cave Gap found its way onto the maps as the Cumberland Gap. Today this natural pathway lies near the spot where Kentucky's southern border meets Virginia and Tennessee.

The First Outpost in Kentucky

Walker pushed ahead, hoping to find flat, fertile land to claim for the Loyal Land Company. The pleasure of finding the pass faded as the horses struggled across a

---

SOURCE DOCUMENT

STAND AT CUMBERLAND GAP, AND WATCH THE PROCESSION OF CIVILIZATION, MARCHING SINGLE FILE—THE BUFFALO FOLLOWING THE TRAIL TO THE SALT SPRINGS, THE INDIAN, THE FUR-TRADER AND HUNTER, THE CATTLE-RAISER, THE FARMER—AND THE FRONTIER HAS PASSED BY. . . . WHEN THE MINES AND THE COW PENS WERE STILL NEAR THE FALL LINE [THE WESTWARD SLOPE OF THE PASS] THE TRADERS' PACK TRAINS WERE TINKLING ACROSS THE ALLEGHANIES, AND THE FRENCH ON THE GREAT LAKES WERE FORTIFYING THEIR POSTS, ALARMED BY THE BRITISH TRADER'S BIRCH CANOES.[7]

In 1893, the brilliant historian Frederick Jackson Turner almost single-handedly revived interest in the westward movement. In these lines from his famous essay, Turner took special note of the importance of the Cumberland Gap. Joining the westward movement, he wrote, exposed settlers to a supreme test of heart and mind. Success was reserved for people like Thomas Walker and Mary Ingles, who were bold, strong, and brave.

chain of wooded valleys. Spirits lifted slightly when Walker found chunks of coal, proof that a coal vein lay close to the surface. When he did find a good piece of bottomland, he ordered his men to build a cabin. The tiny outpost, he said, would guarantee the Loyal Land Company's claim to the land.

While one team cut logs and planted a corn patch, Walker and two companions rode on. Slowed to a crawl by thick woods and brush, Walker climbed a tall tree to see what lay ahead. "As far as my sight could

To mark his claim to Kentucky's fertile land, Thomas Walker ordered his men to build a log cabin and plant a corn patch. Walker's cabin vanished long ago, but modern tourists can relive that historic moment by visiting this replica.

reach," he later wrote, "the land was the same as it had been for the past two days. It was time to turn back."[8]

The trip home went slowly. Poisonous snakes struck several of the horses. A rider injured himself when his mount slipped down a steep bank. It was early July before the expedition reached the frontier settlements. Walker said farewell to his companions and rode back to his family.

Thomas Walker and his party were not the first white men to cross the Cumberland Gap. It was Walker's reports, however, that pinpointed the location and opened the way to Kentucky. Even so, the Loyal Land Company never reaped its hoped-for rewards. Before settlement could go forward, there would be a war to fight and a king's proclamation to overcome. Dr. Walker's next call to duty came during the French and Indian War (1754–63), as Great Britain and France struggled for control of North America. Walker put his talents to work for the British, managing the supply lines for General Edward Braddock's troops. One of the wagon drivers who carted food to the army was a young woodsman named Daniel Boone.

The doctor turned explorer had opened the way, but he could do no more. Twenty-five years later, it was Boone who turned Thomas Walker's dreams into reality.

★ THE GRIM JOURNEY OF MARY INGLES ★

The farmers in eastern Virginia's New River Valley hoped for a good harvest that summer of 1755. Up north, the French and their American Indian allies were taking up arms against British settlers. Down in this lonely settlement, however, all seemed peaceful. Mary Ingles, pregnant with her third child, waved to her husband, William, as he headed out to their fields. Then, with four-year-old Thomas and two-year-old George beside her, she turned to the day's chores.

The attack came with stunning swiftness. A band of Shawnee warriors swept through the cabins, rifles blazing and tomahawks flashing. The handful of settlers fought back, but the Shawnee overwhelmed them. When the

As the frontier pushed westward, American Indian tribes fought to keep their ancestral lands. In this engraving from the mid-1800s, the raiders are Sioux warriors. In Virginia and Kentucky, the attackers often were Shawnee.

raiders left, they took horses, guns, and several prisoners. Among the captives were Mary and her two boys.

The Shawnee soon shook off the militia troops who mounted a tardy pursuit. Then, on the third night out, Ingles went into labor. The next day she climbed back into her saddle, clutching a newborn baby girl in her arms. She knew the warriors would kill her and the baby if she could not keep up. When they reached their camp on the Ohio River, the Shawnee carried Thomas and George off to Detroit. Two-year-old George died on the way. Thomas survived and was adopted by a Shawnee family.

Mary Ingles and her baby were forced to travel with a band of French and Shawnee hunters. The journey took the group to a salt lick in what is now northern Kentucky's Boone County. Ingles earned her captors' trust by taking over some of the camp chores. Along with a second captive, an old Dutch woman, she watched for a chance to escape. One day, while the men were off hunting, the two women told each other that the time had come. It was a painful moment, for Ingles knew she could not survive in the wilderness with a baby in her arms. Her heart ached as she kissed her little girl goodbye and ran from the camp.

For forty days the women struggled through canebrakes, forded streams, and slid down steep hillsides. They lived on berries, nuts, roots, and tender bark. Toward the end of the long journey, hunger drove the Dutch woman a little insane. The old woman wrestled Ingles to the ground and threatened to kill and eat her. With her friend's screams ringing in her ears, Mary Ingles broke loose and fled for her life.

A few days later, Ingles stumbled upon a settler's cabin. The farmer took her in, fed her, and treated her cuts and bruises. After a few days' rest he took her to the nearby fort for a reunion with her husband. As soon as she told the farmer about the old woman, a scouting party went out and found her. The two women hugged each other when they met, their conflict forgotten.

Mary Ingles gave birth to four more children, but she never gave up hope of seeing Thomas again. Eight years later, news came that the boy was alive. William made the long trip to a Shawnee village and bought his son's freedom for $150. The day that Mary welcomed Thomas back into her arms was one of the happiest of her life.

2

WAR COMES TO THE WILDERNESS

Thomas Walker and Mary Ingles walked in the footsteps of Kentucky's earliest peoples. For centuries, tribes of American Indians had sheltered under the region's giant poplar trees and hunted in the grassy meadows. The ancient tribes grew corn, wove fine baskets, and buried their dead in large burial mounds. Hunters pursued game along trails trampled flat by herds of bison. The Warrior's Path carried hunting parties north and south through the Cumberland Gap.

Scientists who dig into the past love to study the people they call the early Mound Builders. From about 800 B.C. to 800 A.D. Mound Builder settlements spread from the Gulf Coast almost to the Great Lakes. The people lived in sturdy, thatched-roof houses and ate a healthy diet of grains, fish, and wild game. An ample food supply gave them time to create their imposing mounds. Crews of workmen built the mounds by piling up rubble and covering it with layers of soil. Tribal artists sometimes topped the mounds with the figures of birds and animals. In Adams County, Ohio, the

Winding through heavy brush across wooded hills, the Warrior's Path once led American Indian warriors to rich hunting grounds beyond the mountains. The narrow path has vanished, but similar trails still wind through Kentucky's state parks.

Great Serpent Mound can be seen from the air as it twists and curls across the countryside.[1]

The first Europeans to reach Kentucky found the settlements deserted. Scientists believe that the Mound Builders left to escape an illness that caused leg and arm bones to soften and break. A lack of critical minerals in the soil may have caused the condition.[2] The heirs to the ancient culture hunted and fished the region, but did not live there. Warfare sometimes erupted when rival hunting bands crossed paths near one of the salt licks. All of the tribes were expert hunters, but some of the northern tribes, such as the Shawnee, did little else. Farther south, the Cherokee lived in villages, grew corn, and fattened animals for food.

Newcomers Upset the Balance

The American Indians lived lightly on the land. Their population numbered in the thousands, not millions. They killed only as much game as they could eat, and cut trees only when they needed to make a canoe or build a shelter. That age-old way of life changed forever when the European newcomers arrived in the 1600s.

Almost from the start, France and England clashed over their conflicting claims to the western lands. In 1668 the great French explorer Robert Cavalier de la Salle paddled down the Ohio River as far as today's Louisville. On a second trip, after reaching the Gulf of Mexico, he took possession of the Mississippi Valley for his king. In 1671, Daumont de Saint-Lusson reinforced la Salle's claim as he stood at the Sault Sainte Marie in Michigan. Speaking to a crowd of American Indians, he announced that France owned everything he could see—as well as all nearby lands, rivers, and lakes.[3]

Farther south, English colonists argued that Virginia stretched from ocean to ocean. The geography of the region worked against this grand claim, however. The Appalachian Mountains cut off the eastern plains from the lands beyond. The few passes that led through the mountains were little known. In the mid-1600s the growth of the fur trade and a surge of land speculation spurred the westward movement. Colonel Abraham Wood trekked inland in 1646 and built Fort Henry on the site of modern Petersburg. From there the British slowly pushed deeper into the wilderness. In 1671 Robert Fallam and Thomas Batts were half starved when they climbed to the top of the ridge that divided the eastern seaboard from the west. Their spirits soared as they stared at lush valleys with streams that ran westward to the Ohio River.

Adventurous hunters, traders, and trappers spent long months adrift in the wilderness, drawn by the splendid hunting. Deep in the Kentucky wilderness Jesse Bledsoe stalked deer that had never heard a gunshot. Often he had time to get off several shots from his flintlock before the survivors fled. When his pile of half-cured hides grew too heavy to carry, Bledsoe hid them near the Cumberland River in southeastern Kentucky. He returned later, only to find that the hides had vanished. To vent his anger, Bledsoe carved the words "2300 deerskins lost, ruination, by God" on a tree trunk.[4]

Gabriel Arthur lived a more exciting adventure. In 1673, while he was visiting the Cherokee, hotheaded young warriors took him captive. His captors wanted to burn him alive, but a friendly chief saved his life. The chief treated young Arthur like an adopted son, and took him on a raid against Spanish settlements in

Knives firmly clasped in their teeth, American Indian hunters close in on a buffalo and small calf. Despite their great size, buffalo were nearly defenseless once they were stampeded into a river.

South Carolina. Later that year, when Arthur was traveling with the Cherokee on a trip north to Ohio, a band of Shawnee attacked. Arthur, slowed by two arrow wounds, again was taken captive. After the Shawnee decided that Arthur really was a white man, they let him go. A long trek down the Warrior's Path from Ohio took the young man back to safety with his Cherokee friends. Safe once more, he kept a promise he had made to the Shawnee. He arranged for English merchants to trade hatchets and flintlocks to the Shawnee in exchange for beaver pelts.

★ *War Comes to the Wilderness* ★

The next chapter in the western movement opened in 1716. That was the year Governor Alexander Spotswood of Virginia crossed the Blue Ridge Mountains at Swift Run Gap (a few miles northeast of present-day Harrisonburg). From that vantage point the fertile Shenandoah Valley spread out before him. In keeping with the custom of the day, Spotswood claimed the entire region for Britain and King George I.

News of the well-watered, fertile soil brought new waves of settlers to the frontier. By 1750 the newcomers had tamed the Shenandoah Valley. Still greedy for elbow room, they now looked beyond the Allegheny Mountains. The sight of the oncoming Virginians alarmed the French and their American Indian allies. Both saw British settlers as a threat to land they claimed as their own.

The French and Indian War

In 1753, Governor Robert Dinwiddie of Virginia sent George Washington to study French-Canadian activities along the frontier. The young surveyor came back with troubling news. The Canadians, he reported, rejected Virginia's claims to the land beyond the mountains. To nail down their own claims, the French were building a chain of forts along the Allegheny and the upper Ohio rivers. At Dinwiddie's orders, Washington returned with a company of militia soldiers. He arrived to find the enemy well dug in at Fort Duquesne (present-day Pittsburgh). Although Washington and his men fought bravely, the outgunned unit was forced

★ 25 ★

to surrender. Because the two nations were not at war, the French allowed the Virginians to return home.

That skirmish helped touch off the long and costly French and Indian War. With their greater numbers, the British expected a quick victory over the French. General Edward Braddock's defeat in 1755 proved otherwise. Unschooled in backwoods tactics, Braddock ignored the advice of Washington and his battle-tested American colonists. While marching on Fort Duquesne, he led his troops down a narrow forest road and into a deadly ambush. The French and their American Indian allies poured volley after volley into the scarlet and blue ranks. Braddock tried to rally his men but was cut down by a well-aimed musket ball. Toward sundown the Redcoats "broke and ran as sheep pursued by dogs," Washington later noted.[5]

For three years the British suffered defeat after defeat in North America. Settlers living on the frontier were forced to drop their plows and flee for their lives. By 1756, the fighting had spread to Europe as well. In a global struggle for supremacy, British and French forces clashed from Canada to India. The tide of battle in North America changed when Prime Minister William Pitt took charge of Britain's war effort. Pitt promoted a corps of talented young officers and sent them to conquer Canada. Fort Duquesne fell in 1758, and Quebec surrendered a year later. When Montreal fell, the French knew they were beaten. In 1763, France gave up Canada and its claims to the vast territory east of the Mississippi River.

A New Barrier: The Proclamation of 1763

The peace treaty did not end the fighting. American Indian leaders warned their people that their way of life was threatened by new waves of British settlers. The oncoming tide already had driven many eastern tribes from their lands. The only answer, the tribes agreed, was to fight back. War parties carried out savage hit-and-run raids along the frontier. Each time they struck, the warriors took a fierce vengeance on the settlers and their families.

The fresh onslaught forced British officials to rethink the future. Why fight a costly war with the American Indians when there was land aplenty east of the mountains? Victory over France and its allies had brought vast new territories under the British flag. The western tribes could be dealt with, the officials argued, after the eastern territories were fully settled. To enforce the new policy, King George III barred settlement west of the Appalachians when he signed the Proclamation of 1763. Instead of looking west, settlers were ordered to move north to Nova Scotia or south to Georgia.

Safe in his London palace, the king was out of touch with events in the New World. American colonists enjoyed greater freedoms—of speech, press, and assembly—than did their cousins in Britain. When faced with limits on their liberties, Americans rebelled. One of those rights, they argued, was the freedom to make one's own way in the world. Out on the frontier, people were judged by what they could do, not who

PROCLAMATION OF 1763

AND WE DO FURTHER DECLARE IT TO BE OUR ROYAL WILL AND PLEASURE, . . . TO RESERVE UNDER OUR SOVEREIGNTY, PROTECTION, AND DOMINION, FOR THE USE OF THE SAID INDIANS, ALL THE LAND AND TERRITORIES NOT INCLUDED WITHIN THE LIMITS OF OUR . . . NEW GOVERNMENTS, . . . AS ALSO ALL THE LAND AND TERRITORIES LYING TO THE WESTWARD OF THE SOURCES OF THE RIVERS WHICH FALL INTO THE SEA FROM THE WEST AND NORTHWEST AS AFORESAID; AND WE DO HEREBY STRICTLY FORBID, ON PAIN OF OUR DISPLEASURE, ALL OUR LOVING SUBJECTS FROM MAKING ANY PURCHASES OR SETTLEMENTS WHATEVER, OR TAKING POSSESSION OF ANY OF THE LANDS ABOVE RESERVED, WITHOUT OUR SPECIAL LEAVE AND LICENSE FOR THAT PURPOSE FIRST OBTAINED.

AND WE DO FURTHER STRICTLY ENJOIN AND REQUIRE ALL PERSONS WHATEVER, WHO HAVE EITHER WILFULLY OR INADVERTENTLY SEATED THEMSELVES UPON ANY LANDS WITHIN THE COUNTRIES ABOVE DESCRIBED, OR UPON ANY OTHER LANDS WHICH, NOT HAVING BEEN CEDED TO OR PURCHASED BY US, ARE STILL RESERVED TO THE SAID INDIANS AS AFORESAID, FORTHWITH TO REMOVE THEMSELVES FROM SUCH SETTLEMENTS.[6]

After the French and Indian War, Americans hoped to open the west to settlement. They soon learned that the British government had other ideas. Alarmed by reports of clashes between settlers and the American Indian tribes, King George III issued the Proclamation of 1763. In the stilted language of the day, he ordered the colonists to confine their settlements to the lands east of the Allegheny Mountains. His not-so-loving subjects soon found ways to evade this unwelcome order.

they were. Did you shoot straight? How well did you swing an axe? Could you plow, plant, and harvest? Those were the skills that counted.

Land hunger fueled the surge westward. Tobacco planters found to their dismay that their popular crop soon exhausted newly cleared fields. Immigrants were arriving in greater numbers as well. As the settled areas filled up, the newcomers sought land they could claim as their own. An Irish immigrant named Polly Mulhollin was one of them. Mulhollin worked off the cost of her passage, then headed into the woods. Building a cabin on virgin land, she knew, entitled her to claim the surrounding hundred acres. She built her first cabin—and kept on going. In all, she put up thirty cabins in the Shenandoah Valley—and won title to the land that went with each one.[7]

The westward surge was further driven by land speculation. Armed with huge western land grants, speculators hoped to enrich themselves by selling their claims. George Washington's Mississippi Company held the rights to 2.5 million acres in the Mississippi Valley. When Thomas Walker built his cabin in Kentucky, he was staking out a claim on behalf of the Loyal Land Company. Soldiers lately returned from service in the French and Indian War made up a second group of speculators. Many had been paid with paper certificates called warrants that could be traded in for acreage out west. Now, with the war over, the men were determined to take what was theirs. The king's officers protested, but they were unable to enforce the Proclamation of 1763.

As the land hunger mounted, colonial officials held meetings with American Indian leaders. The most notable congress took place in 1768 at Fort Stanwix in New York's Mohawk Valley. After days of talks, the Iroquois signed over a vast territory to the British colonial officials, including all rights to Kentucky. In return, the British promised to keep settlers out of Iroquois lands north of the Ohio River. That same year, the Cherokee signed a similar treaty that they

From its origins in eastern Kentucky, the Kentucky River flows northeast to empty into the Ohio River. Daniel Boone settled near here after he cut the Wilderness Road north from the Cumberland Gap.

hoped would safeguard their lands in the south. This treaty, too, left Kentucky open to settlement.

Down in the Yadkin Valley of North Carolina, Daniel Boone was catching a bad case of Kentucky fever. Over the next twenty years he would leave his stamp on history as explorer, hunter, soldier—and road-builder.

★ A HOUSE FIT FOR WILDERNESS LIVING[8] ★

America's early colonists built houses like the ones they knew in the Old Country. English farmers put up simple frame houses sided with weatherboards. Well-to-do Dutch merchants raised their families in sturdy brick houses. As settlers moved into the wilderness, they met a new challenge. To build English-style frame houses, they needed well-seasoned lumber and costly iron nails. Neither was easy to come by on the frontier.

By the time Thomas Walker journeyed west in 1750, most settlers were living in what Walker called "Indian cabins." The term "log cabin" appeared later. Swedish immigrants brought the know-how for building these snug homes with them. The woods furnished the building materials, and a team of axmen could raise a log cabin almost overnight. The simplest technique fitted rows of notched round logs one on top of another. If they had time, the men would hew (square off) the logs at top and bottom to make a tighter fit.

Walker's friend Samuel Stalnaker put up a cabin made from round logs. The trader had already prepared the foundation—four partly hewn logs arranged in a square. Walker put his three best axmen to work beside Stalnaker. Their task was to notch the logs and fit them together.

The other two men harnessed their horses to drag new logs to the building site. That left Walker free to chink the cabin, to protect it from harsh weather.

The work went quickly. A workman stood at each corner of the cabin, axe in hand. When a log arrived, he cut notches at both ends, one notch on top and one on the bottom. When the logs were levered into place, the notches locked them together without nails or pegs. Walker chinked the cabin by stuffing twigs and moss into the cracks before sealing the seams with wet clay. When the clay dried, the cabin would be weatherproof.

By noon the work crew had raised the four walls. After a break to rest and eat, the men chopped a doorway

The pioneers' first task after reaching their destination was to erect a palisade of sharpened timbers. For cooking, the women hung iron pots on tripods made from tree limbs.

through one side of the cabin. Next they cut a second opening for a fireplace, then went to work building a shingled roof. If Stalnaker had planned to bring his family there, he would have put down a wooden floor. For now, he was content to live with a hard-packed dirt floor.

Stalnaker's log cabin went on to earn a modest bit of fame. In 1755 a map drawn by Lewis Evans labeled the cabin as "the furthest settlement in Virginia." Walker saw it for the last time when he rode away on March 26, 1750. Ahead lay the path that would take him to the Cumberland Gap.

3

"EVERY HEART ABOUNDED WITH JOY"

In 1728 William Byrd II trekked into the wilderness to survey the border between Virginia and North Carolina. Like most gentlemen of his day, Byrd took a pack train of creature comforts with him. He hired American Indians to do his hunting and his servants came along to cook his meals. This "beef-and-biscuit" Englishman washed his supper down with a good wine and slept in a tent. In his report, Byrd noted: "The chief discouragement at present from penetrating far into the woods is the trouble of carrying a load of provisions. . . . But the common precautions against [famine] are so burthensome, that people cannot . . . go far enough from home, to make any effectual discovery."[1]

Byrd failed to notice that a new breed of American already stalked the woods beyond the frontier settlements. These were the "long hunters," named for their lengthy forays into the wilderness in pursuit of furs and hides. Farm work bored these tough, resourceful men. Each year they left their homes and families while they gave themselves over to the thrill of the chase. The long hunters practiced the same woodcraft that American Indian hunters knew so well. Keen-eyed and alert, they learned to read the signs left by deer, bears, buffalo, and other game. Each broken branch, footprint, and pile of droppings told a useful tale.

When Thomas Walker rode west in 1750 his wool clothing marked him for what he was—a planter, not a long hunter. Except for his moccasins, Walker would have blended in with the townsfolk of Williamsburg. The true long hunters wore deerskin hunting shirts belted at the waist. Most favored raccoon caps with tails hanging behind. Like the hunters, Walker relied on his long rifle for food. His final journal entry proves that he and his men knew how to shoot: "We killed on the journey 13 buffaloes, 8 elks, 53 bears, 20 deer, 4 wild geese, about 150 turkeys, besides small game. We might have killed three times as much meat if we wanted it."[2]

"Daniel Will Do the Shooting"

The footprints of English and French hunters and traders crisscrossed Kentucky long before Daniel Boone arrived. It remained for this great long hunter, however, to open Kentucky to settlement. In doing so, Boone carved out a place for himself among the heroes of the western movement. One admirer later termed him "the Prince of Pioneers."

Daniel's grandfather, George Boone, left England to settle near Philadelphia in 1717. Within the year he moved westward to a farm near present-day Reading,

Pennsylvania. His son Squire grew up there, married, and farmed the land. Large families were common in those days, and Squire welcomed his sixth son, Daniel, in 1734. Because the Boone farm lay at the edge of the wilderness, young Daniel Boone spent more time in the woods than he did in school. The Delaware and Shawnee hunters who stopped by to visit taught him to "think like an Indian." Those lessons saved him more than once in the years that followed. When his uncle complained that the boy was a poor speller, Squire had a ready response. "Let the girls do the spelling," he said, "and Daniel will do the shooting."[3]

In 1748 Squire moved his family south to a 640-acre farm in North Carolina. Daniel, always a free spirit, now spent more and more time in the woods. He hunted deer, turkey, and bear with Tick Licker, his long-barreled flintlock rifle. When the French and Indian War broke out, Daniel signed on as a wagon driver with the British Army. During the campaign he met John Finley, who described for him the wonders of Kentucky.

After Braddock's crushing defeat, the young man went home to the Yadkin Valley in western North Carolina. There he married Rebecca Bryan and took up a life of farming and hunting. By the mid-1760s, however, Boone was feeling restless. More settlers were moving into the valley, and game was growing scarce. In 1769, John Finley stopped by the Boone cabin and rekindled Daniel's interest in Kentucky. As historian John Bakeless wrote, "The Boones were wanderers born. They had the itching foot. . . . They heard of distant lands and knew that they must go there."[4]

Boone's First Foray into Kentucky

A few weeks later, Boone led a party of friends through the Cumberland Gap. For six months the men hunted and trapped in the unspoiled wilderness. Then trouble arrived in the form of a Shawnee war party. The Shawnee overran the men's camp and stole their horses, furs, and deer hides. The Shawnee leader let the hunters go with a warning. "If you are so foolish as to venture here again," he said, "the wasps and yellow jackets will sting you severely."[5] Later, Boone and his brother-in-law stole back their horses, only to be recaptured. This time the hunters were lucky to escape with their lives.

Boone refused to quit. He picked up fresh supplies and continued his long hunt. Soon he knew how to find each hill, stream, and salt lick over a wide stretch of Kentucky countryside. On the way home in 1771, trouble struck again. This time it was a band of Cherokee who stole the furs and hides he had gathered. Boone arrived home broke and in debt, but nothing could spoil his love for the land beyond the mountains.

Two years later, Boone bundled up Rebecca and his eight children and led a group of settlers into Kentucky. Burdened with small children and livestock, the party moved slowly. When food ran low Boone dispatched his son James and some other men to bring back fresh supplies. A few nights later a war party of Delaware Indians opened fire on the supply train. The

When Richard Henderson needed a road cut through the wilderness to Kentucky, he hired Daniel Boone (shown here) for the job. The famous long hunter and his party of woodsmen blazed a narrow trail that crossed through the Cumberland Gap before turning north to the Kentucky River.

deadly rifle balls killed two men and wounded James and one of his friends. Daniel Boone reached the scene a day later, but he was too late to save his son. The raiders had tortured and killed the helpless teenagers.

News of the massacre took the heart out of the settlers. Boone buried his son and returned home with the others. In the brief war that followed the attack, he took command of several frontier forts. His leadership helped save the settlements, but when the fighting ended his creditors took him to court. As the court cases dragged on, Boone struck up a friendship with lawyer Richard Henderson. The two men talked about Kentucky, and how to open it to settlement. Henderson worked out a plan to buy 20 million acres from the Cherokee. Once the land was his, he felt sure, he would make a fortune selling farm plots to eager settlers.

The Treaty of Sycamore Shoals

Henderson was not troubled by the fact that the Cherokee did not own the land he wanted to buy. Neither did he and his partners worry about breaking British law by moving settlers west of the mountains. To tempt the Cherokee, Henderson loaded a dozen wagons with trade goods—guns, whiskey, flour, cheap trinkets, woolen shirts, and iron tools. Boone did his part by setting up a meeting with the main Cherokee chiefs. When Henderson reached Sycamore Shoals, Tennessee, in March 1775, over a thousand Cherokee were waiting to greet him.

After much bargaining, the Cherokee chiefs signed a deal that paid them trade goods and cash worth some ten thousand English pounds. In return, Henderson gained the rights to all the land that lay south of the Ohio River between the Cumberland and Kentucky Rivers. The chiefs also signed a "path deed" that gave Henderson the right to cut a road through to his land. The treaty angered some of the more thoughtful Cherokee, including a much-respected chief named Oconostota. The proud old man looked into the future and cautioned,

> This is but the beginning. . . . The invader has crossed the great sea in ships; he has not been stayed by broad rivers, and now he has penetrated the wilderness and overcome the ruggedness of the mountains. . . . He will force the Indian steadily before him across the Mississippi ever towards the west . . . till the red man be no longer a roamer of the forests and a pursuer of wild game.[6]

The words fell on deaf ears. Most of the Cherokee were eager to begin sharing out the trade goods.

Chief Dragging Canoe added his own warning. As he reminded Boone, the tribes to the west and north had not shared in the treaty. "You have bought a fair land," he said, "but there is a dark cloud hanging over it." In years to come, settlers had good reason to remember Dragging Canoe's advice. Thanks to the Shawnee and other warlike tribes, Kentucky soon earned a new nickname—"the dark and bloody ground."[7]

IT WAS THE FIRST OF MAY, IN THE YEAR 1769, THAT I RESIGNED MY DOMESTIC HAPPINESS FOR A TIME AND LEFT . . . TO WANDER . . . IN QUEST OF THE COUNTRY OF KENTUCKE, IN COMPANY WITH JOHN FINLEY, JOHN STEWART, JOSEPH HOLDEN, JAMES MONAY, AND WILLIAM COOL. [A]FTER A LONG AND FATIGUING JOURNEY THROUGH A MOUNTAINOUS WILDERNESS, . . . ON THE SEVENTH DAY OF JUNE FOLLOWING WE FOUND OURSELVES ON RED RIVER . . . AND, FROM THE TOP OF AN EMINENCE, SAW WITH PLEASURE THE BEAUTIFUL LEVEL [PLAINS] OF KENTUCKE.

WE FOUND EVERYWHERE ABUNDANCE OF WILD BEASTS OF ALL SORTS THROUGH THIS VAST FOREST. THE BUFFALOES WERE MORE FREQUENT THAN I HAVE SEEN CATTLE IN THE SETTLEMENTS, BROWSING ON THE LEAVES OF THE CANE, OR CROPPING THE HERBAGE ON THOSE EXTENSIVE PLAINS, FEARLESS, BECAUSE IGNORANT, OF THE VIOLENCE OF MAN. SOMETIMES WE SAW HUNDREDS IN A DROVE, AND THE NUMBERS ABOUT THE SALT SPRINGS WERE AMAZING. . . .

ONE DAY I UNDERTOOK A TOUR THROUGH THE COUNTRY, AND THE DIVERSITY AND BEAUTIES OF NATURE I MET WITH IN THIS CHARMING SEASON EXPELLED EVERY GLOOMY AND VEXATIOUS THOUGHT. I LAID ME DOWN TO SLEEP, AND I AWOKE NOT UNTIL THE SUN HAD CHASED AWAY THE NIGHT. I CONTINUED THIS TOUR, AND IN A FEW DAYS EXPLORED A CONSIDERABLE PART OF THE COUNTRY, EACH DAY EQUALLY PLEASED AS THE FIRST.[8]

Daniel Boone was far too busy to sit down and write his own story. Luckily he did talk to John Filson about his early days in Kentucky. In 1784, Filson printed his version of Boone's adventures as part of a longer book on the discovery and settlement of Kentucky. When asked if Filson's stories were true, Boone winked and replied, "All true! . . . Not a lie in it!"[9]

A Road Across the Mountains

Henderson's dream of founding a fourteenth American colony called Transylvania now seemed within reach. As a first step he hired Boone to blaze a road across the mountains. Boone rode back to the Yadkin Valley and rounded up a party of thirty North Carolina axmen. Recruits were easy to find, for he offered good pay—ten English pounds and a tract of land along the Kentucky River. Boone's own agreement with Henderson included a bounty of two thousand acres.

No one seemed to worry that the new road must cross two hundred miles of wilderness. The men sang and joked as they left Long Island in northeastern Tennessee on March 10, 1775. Young Felix Walker was one of those who could hardly wait to begin the great adventure. He wrote in his journal that, "every heart abounded with joy and excitement in anticipating the new things we could see, and the romantic scenes through which we must pass; . . . the settlement of a new country was a dazzling object with many of our company."[10]

The first miles led along a well-traveled wagon road. The easy going ended near the Virginia border at Moccasin Gap. There the men turned onto a narrow, overgrown trail. Boone rode ahead, blazing the trees that marked the route. Behind him, the axmen cleared away brush, vines, and small trees. Other workmen dragged fallen trees out of the way, burned dead brush, and cut through the canebrakes. Swift-flowing

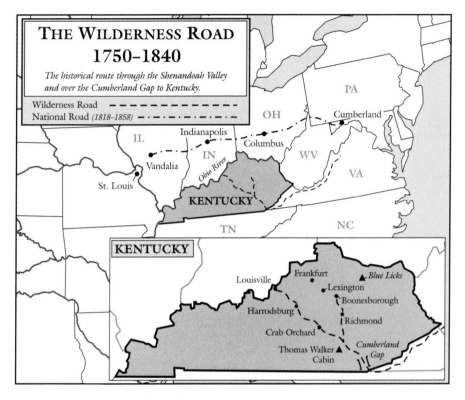

Boone's Trace branched north to Boonesborough, but later travelers preferred the easier route through Crab Orchard and Harrodsburg. The Wilderness Road reigned as the prime east-west pathway until the wider, smoother National Road opened for business in the early 1800s.

streams, freezing rain, snow, and ankle-deep mud slowed their progress, but the men slogged on. They named one stream Troublesome Creek because it gave them so much grief. At night they huddled around campfires and cooked the wild game Boone shot during the day.

The route led through Virginia's Clinch River valley and over a mountain to the valley of the Powell

River. At Rose Hill, Boone found Joseph Martin hard at work rebuilding a settlement abandoned after a Cherokee raid in 1769. The road-builders rested there and restocked their food stores. The next leg of the trip went quickly, for a well-used trail led to the Cumberland Gap. After passing through the gap, the road-builders knew they were in Kentucky.

Boone turned northwest to follow the Warrior's Path. This "buffalo road," which the herds had long ago trampled flat, gave the tired axmen a welcome break. Because buffalo seldom traveled in a straight line, the road meandered crazily. The men complained about creeks "that we crost about 50 times [over] some very bad foards."[11]

After crossing the Rockcastle River, the path plunged into miles of dense brush and thick cane. On March 22, after days of backbreaking work, the party came out of the hills. The men whooped and hollered as they gazed across rolling plains covered with clover in full bloom. Some ten miles farther on, Boone gave orders to make camp at a site near present-day Richmond. The land that would later be called "the smiling lands of the Bluegrass" lay less than two days away.

That night the weary road-builders felt certain that their labors were almost over. This was their land, fairly bought and paid for! The woods were quiet as the men curled up in their blankets. No one thought to post a guard.

★ DANIEL BOONE ★
By Arthur Cuiterman[12]

I

Daniel Boone at twenty-one
Came with his tomahawk, knife, and gun
Home from the French and Indian War
To North Carolina and the Yadkin shore.
He married his maid with a golden band,
Builded his house and cleared his land;
But the deep woods claimed their son again
And he turned his face from the homes of men.
Over the Blue Ridge, dark and lone,
The Mountains of Iron, the Hills of Stone,
Braving the Shawnee's jealous wrath,
He made his way on the Warrior's Path.
Alone he trod the shadowed trails;
But he was lord of a thousand vales
As he roved Kentucky, far and near,
Hunting the buffalo, elk, and deer.
What joy to see, what joy to win
So fair a land for his kith and kin.
Of streams unstained and woods unhewn!
"Elbow room!" laughed Daniel Boone.

II

On the Wilderness Road that his axmen made
The settlers flocked to the first stockade;
The deerskin shirts and the coonskin caps
Filed through the glens and the mountain gaps;
And hearts were high in the fateful spring
When the land say "Nay" to the stubborn king.
While the men of the East of farm and town
Strove with the troops of the British Crown,
Daniel Boone from a surge of hate
Guarded a nation's westward gate.
Down in the fort in a wave of flame
The Shawnee horde and the Mingo came,
And the stout logs shook in a storm of lead;
But Boone stood firm and the savage fled.

★ 45 ★

Peace! And the settlers flocked anew,
The farm lands spread, the town lands grew;
But Daniel Boone was ill at ease
When he saw the smoke in his forest trees.
"There'll be no game in the country soon.
Elbow room!" cried Daniel Boone.

III

Straight as a pine at sixty-five
Time enough for a man to thrive
He launched his bateau on Ohio's breast
And his heart was glad as he oared it west;
There were kindly folk and his own true blood
Where great Missouri rolls his flood;
New woods, new streams, and room to spare,
And Daniel Boone found comfort there.
Yet far he ranged toward the sunset still,
Where the Kansas runs and the Smoky Hill,
And the prairies toss, by the south wind blown;
And he killed his bear on the Yellowstone.
But ever he dreamed of new domains
With vast woods and wider plains;
Ever he dreamed of a world-to-be
Where there are no bounds and the soul is free.
At fourscore-five, still stout and hale,
He heard a call to a farther trail;
So he turned his face where the stars are strewn;
"Elbow room!" sighed Daniel Boone.

Arthur Cuiterman's poetic tribute to Daniel Boone emphasizes the great woodsman's noble spirit and heroic achievements. As the poet notes, Boone never stopped yearning for elbow room—but that was not the only reason he left Kentucky. Time after time, the courts ruled against the aging woodsman when newcomers challenged his land titles.

THE LONG, HARD ROAD

On the night of March 24, 1775, Daniel Boone awoke to the sounds of gunshots and Shawnee war cries. As his men scrambled for their weapons, William Twitty screamed and went down. Musket balls had shattered both of his knees. Sam, the wounded man's African-American servant, fell into the fire, mortally wounded. Two warriors ran forward to take their victims' scalps, but were driven back by Twitty's bulldog. In the confusion, as the Shawnee struggled to tomahawk the dog, Boone and the other road-builders fled with their wounded. The raiders left almost as quickly, taking only a few horses.

The surprise attack unnerved several of the men. While they packed up to leave for home, Boone put the others to work building a crude fort. When Twitty died two days later, the men buried him next to Sam and named the fort in his honor. Felix Walker seemed certain to die of his wounds, but Boone refused to give up hope. The grateful young man wrote in his journal, "He attended me as his child, cured my wounds by the use of medicines from the woods, and nursed me . . . until I recovered."[1]

With supplies running low, Boone sent out a hunting party. Two nights later the Shawnee fired on the hunters as they dried their moccasins in front of a campfire. The gunfire cut down two of the men and sent the survivors fleeing for the shelter of Twitty's Fort. Boone wrote a report and dispatched a rider to deliver it to Richard Henderson. The messenger found Henderson's pack train camped twenty miles east of Cumberland Gap. In his note, Boone urged Henderson to press on as quickly as possible, "for the people are very uneasy." This is the time, he advised, "to flusterate [the Indians'] intentions and keep the country, whilst we are in it. If we give way to them now, it will ever be the case."[2]

After resting a few days, Boone and his road-builders pushed on to the Kentucky River. There, in a sheltered hollow the men called Boonesborough, the segment of the Wilderness Road that Boone and his men had blazed came to an end. With memories of four new graves spurring them on, the men hurried to build a fort. Henderson and his party arrived on April 20. Cheered by the sight of reinforcements, the little band welcomed him with a salute of rifle fire.

For a moment, the future looked bright. All across Kentucky, new settlements were taking root. Henderson did not know that his dream of founding a new colony would die during the coming Revolutionary War. Nor did the settlers know that a separate "Indian war" had started that would last seven long, bloody years.

Kentucky's pioneer families turned frontier outposts such as Boonesborough into well-fortified strongpoints. Stout walls, with blockhouses at each corner (top) helped protect settlers from American Indian raiders. Within the walls (bottom), the people of Boonesborough thrived in sturdy log cabins.

On cold evenings, settlers sought warmth and companionship in front of their fireplaces. After eating stew cooked in iron pots, families gathered before the fire to talk about the events of the day.

A No-Holds-Barred Conflict

As Dragging Canoe had warned, the Shawnee, the Wyandot, and other neighboring tribes tried to drive out the newcomers. The Cherokee, even though they had signed the treaty of Sycamore Shoals, joined in the struggle. For the American Indians, the issue was clear. If they did not fight, white settlers would overrun their hunting grounds. In the troubled months that followed, war parties left behind a trail of mangled bodies and burning cabins.

The thirteen-star flag that flies outside Old Fort Harrod State Park reminds visitors that time has been frozen here. The rebuilt fort stands on the site where James Harrod founded Kentucky's first permanent white settlement.

The raids sent some settlers hurrying to safety east of the Cumberland Gap. Others left lonely cabins and half-cleared fields to take shelter in Kentucky's larger settlements. Despite the danger, Boone and dozens of others retraced their steps, packed up their families, and returned to Kentucky over the new road. They knew they were on their own. With the American Revolution heating up, the hard-pressed eastern colonies could do little to help them. To make matters worse, several American Indian tribes had allied themselves with the British. Now they turned their British weapons on the new settlements.

The settlers at Boonesborough kept watch, but their foes moved like shadows through the woods. In July 1776, a Cherokee band kidnapped Boone's daughter Jemima and two of her teenage friends. Boone led the pursuit, guided by the bits of cloth and broken twigs the girls left behind. The rescuers caught up with the raiders two days later, forty miles from Boonesborough. Secure in the belief that they had escaped, the Cherokee had stopped to roast a buffalo. Caught off guard, they fled when the settlers closed in and opened fire. A few anxious moments later, Boone was holding Jemima in his arms.[3]

The war grew more deadly as the months passed. For good reason, the settlers later spoke of 1777 as the Year of the Bloody Sevens. From his stronghold at Detroit, a British governor known as the "hair buyer" paid bounties for American scalps. He also offered pardons and land grants to settlers who switched to the British side. The offer drew few takers, even though the American Indians were stepping up their attacks.

Boonesborough was hit three times that year, and Harrodsburg came under siege twice. Cut off from supplies, the settlers dressed in rags. When raiders burned their fields, they sometimes went hungry. At Boonesborough, the women made do with a coarse cloth woven from buffalo hair and fibers taken from wild nettles.[4] Hunters slipped in and out of the fort at night, ever alert for lurking war parties.

Daniel Boone and a rescue party open fire on the Cherokee warriors who kidnapped Jemima Boone and two other teenagers. The resourceful girls helped their own cause by leaving behind a trail of broken twigs and bits of clothing for Boone to follow.

At Logan's Fort, Shawnee raiders ambushed a group of women who had left the stockade to milk their cattle. The women escaped, but rifle fire killed one of their guards and wounded another. Benjamin Logan somehow evaded a hail of bullets as he dashed out to carry the injured man to safety. Simon Kenton performed a similar feat at Boonesborough. The drama began when a band of Shawnee caught Boone, Kenton, and ten of their friends outside the walls. Boone led an all-or-nothing charge through the Shawnee, only to fall when a rifle ball shattered his ankle. Kenton spun around and shot a warrior who was reaching for Boone's scalp. He crushed a second Shawnee skull with his gun barrel, hoisted Boone to his shoulders, and ran to the fort.

As the Revolution dragged on, a British officer carried out the bloodiest raids of the long war. Riding at the head of a Shawnee war party, Henry Bird used a cannon to batter down the walls of two small forts. After the settlers surrendered, he turned them over to the Shawnee to be massacred. George Rogers Clark repaid the debt by leading an expedition against the British and their Shawnee allies. His victories in Illinois and at Chillicothe, Ohio, helped relieve the pressure on Kentucky's settlers. In 1782 the settlers stumbled into a final defeat at the Battle of Blue Licks in northern Kentucky, but the worst was over. Kentucky fever burned bright as new waves of settlers packed their gear for the trip over the Wilderness Road.

A Daunting Challenge

Settlers headed for Kentucky gathered at a Virginia jumping-off point known as the Block House. Ahead lay some 225 miles of narrow, twisting road. From the Block House the road ran northwest for 35 miles and climbed two mountains to reach the Powell Valley. The next leg turned west for 45 miles, rising at last to the Cumberland Gap and the travelers' first steps on Kentucky soil. Fifteen miles north of the gap, the road cut through a pass at Pine Mountain and forded the

Cumberland River. From that point settlers threaded their way northwest for a hundred hard-won miles.

The final miles brought them to the plains of central Kentucky and a fork in the road. A few hardy souls turned north on Boone's Trace to Boonesborough, Winchester, and Lexington. Most took the easier route that led west to Crab Orchard (named for the crab apples that grew wild there), Logan's Station (today's Stanford), and Harrodsburg.[5]

Each mile offered a new challenge. The pioneers had to climb mountains, wade across swift-flowing streams, and splash across boggy meadows. Back in 1775, Richard Henderson spoke for the thousands who would follow in Boone's footsteps. "No part of the road [was] tolerable," he wrote, "most of it either hilly, stony, slippery, miry [muddy], or bushy."[6] Despite those obstacles, horsemen sometimes made amazingly good time. In 1782, William Brown and eleven friends left the Block House for Kentucky. They reached the Dix River south of Crab Orchard just seven days later.

In the early years, the Wilderness Road was known by several names. Some called it "the Road to Caintuck." Others knew it as "the Great Western Road" or "the Kentucky Path."[7] By any name, the pioneers who set foot on the road knew that it would test their courage, skill, and endurance. Until work crews widened the road to thirty feet in 1795, wagons had to be left east of the Cumberland Gap. The settlers loaded their household goods onto packhorses and rode or

George Rogers Clark planned his Revolutionary War campaigns from a wooden desk at Old Fort Harrod. In 1778, with a force of only 175 men, he marched north to Illinois and overran several British forts. Four years later, General Clark relieved pressure on Kentucky's settlers by defeating the Shawnee at Chillicothe, Ohio.

walked in single file. Despite these hardships, at least seventy thousand people traveled the Wilderness Road between 1775 and 1795.

In 1781 the war between the settlers and the American Indians spread eastward. Cherokee raiders slashed at pack trains as they passed between the Block House and Cumberland Gap. The danger subsided after a militia force marched into Cherokee country and razed three towns. The soldiers also rescued fifteen captives, including a number of children. At the same time, westbound settlers improved their odds by joining larger groups. More men meant more guns—and less chance of being attacked along the way. As late as 1788, this notice appeared in the *Kentucky Gazette*: "A large company will meet at the Crab Orchard the 19th of November in order to start the next day through the Wilderness. As it is very dangerous on account of the Indians, it is hoped each person will go well armed."[8]

SOURCE DOCUMENT

CAN ANYTHING BE MORE ABSURD THAN THE CONDUCT OF MAN? HERE IS HUNDREDS TRAVELLING HUNDREDS OF MILES, THEY KNOW NOT FOR WHAT NOR WHITHER, EXCEPT ITS TO KENTUCKEY, PASSING LAND ALMOST AS GOOD AND EASY OBTAINED . . . BUT IT WILL NOT DO, ITS NOT KENTUCKEY, ITS NOT THE PROMISED LAND, ITS NOT THE GOODLY INHERATENCE, THE LAND OF MILK AND HONEY.

—MOSES AUSTIN, *A MEMORANDUM* . . . 1796–97[9]

The settlers who traveled west on the Wilderness Road paid little heed to these harsh words. For them, Kentucky was the land of milk and honey. Austin most likely penned this comment after he passed through the territory on his way to Missouri. Later, after his mining business failed, he enlisted his son Stephen in a plan to open Texas to American settlers. The older man died before realizing his dream, but Stephen went on to enduring fame as a leader of the Texas independence movement. A grateful people named the state capital Austin in his honor.

Traveling the Wilderness Road

Colonel James Knox led a typical pack train over the Wilderness Road in 1784. After a preacher gave the departing Virginians his blessing, the settlers said good-bye to friends and relatives. As each family fell into line, everyone kept a watchful eye on children, livestock, and the heavily loaded horses. The horses carried pack saddles from which hung large woven baskets. The baskets were piled high with dried foods, farming tools, cooking gear, bedding, clothing, and furniture. Parents also made room in the baskets for small children. Those families that owned Bibles packed them with special care.

Knox's party grew in size as it moved westward. At Bean's Station in Tennessee, nearly two hundred settlers from North Carolina joined the Virginians. As the wilderness closed in and the danger of Cherokee raids increased, Knox organized advance and rear guards. By this time the single file line of march stretched back nearly two miles along the trail. At Clinch Mountain in northern Tennessee the steep grade defeated some of the packhorses. The men were forced to haul the packs up on their backs.

The ford across the Clinch River proved to be just as challenging. A woman tried to cross the river with a baby in her arms and a child riding behind her, but the current nearly swept her away. Holding tight to the baby with one hand, she clutched the bridle with the other. Her firm grip kept the horse swimming toward the opposite bank. As she neared shore, strong hands

This famous painting by George Caleb Bingham is called, Daniel Boone Escorting Settlers Through the Cumberland Gap. *The painter portrayed the heroic woodsman leading a caravan, his rifle resting on his shoulder.*

pulled the exhausted mother and the frightened children to safety.

Knox posted guards that night, for scouts had found signs that Cherokee were nearby. The next morning eight men rode past, traveling fast and light. Knox warned them of the danger, but the strangers waved and pressed onward. Later that day, the advance guard found the eight horsemen. All were dead. Their assailants had scalped them and left the bodies for the wolves to feed on. Knox gave orders to bury the men, and the settlers said a prayer for their souls.

Each day seemed to bring new miseries. Cattle wandered away and had to be rounded up. Pack saddles pulled loose, spilling their loads along the road. At night the howling of wolves and the hooting of owls kept nerves on edge. Everyone knew that American Indians used animal calls to signal an attack. Sudden rains turned to sleet and snow. The road melted into a quagmire, and streams overflowed their banks. Horses went lame, leaving their riders to limp along on blistered feet. Worst of all, an outbreak of measles hit the company. Knox rode up and down the line, doing his best to keep spirits high. Over and over he assured worried mothers that they would soon be out of the wilderness.

The weary settlers straggled into Crab Orchard on November 1. Knox said his farewells there, his duty done. He told his new friends that he admired their courage and patience. Before riding away he added, "I hope you will find in this new country happy homes, and long may you enjoy its blessings and abundance!"[10]

★ THE KENTUCKY LONG RIFLE ★

During the Revolution, British troops complained that Americans did not fight fair. Firing from hidden positions in the woods was bad enough. What really upset the Redcoats was the accurate, long-range fire laid down by their foes. British smoothbore muskets had an effective range of under a hundred yards. American sharpshooters, by contrast, picked off British officers at two hundred yards.

The gun that helped win the Revolution was known as the Kentucky long rifle. The rifle was born in the 1730s when German gunsmiths began cutting spiral grooves inside the barrels of their new guns. The grooves (also called rifles, a term that gave the guns their name) spun the lead bullet as it was fired. Instead of tumbling through the air, the spinning ball flew straight and true. Hunters also treasured the long rifle for its light weight and its thrifty use of lead and powder.

Early riflemen rammed a lead ball (the bullet) into the barrel with a metal ramrod. All too often, the hammering ruined the shape of the bullet and spoiled the shot. As time went on, men switched to smaller balls and wrapped them in greased patches before ramming them home. The cloth patch engaged the rifle grooves and kept the ball true and round. The patch also kept the ball from rolling out if a hunter tilted the gun downward.

A skilled rifleman could load and fire a .38-caliber Kentucky rifle with surprising speed. The hunter first poured a measured amount of gunpowder into the barrel. Next he rammed the ball home, sprinkled powder in the firing pan, closed the cover, and cocked the hammer. When he pulled the trigger, the hammer fell, striking a spark that ignited the powder in the firing pan. The superheated air blasted through the touchhole and exploded the powder inside the barrel. An instant later the expanding gases sent the ball spinning on its way. Misfires were frequent. The usual culprits were damp powder, a dull flint, or a clogged touchhole. Wise hunters lived by the rule, "Keep your powder dry."

Long hunters were jokingly said to have treated their rifles better than they did their wives. True or not, most thought of their guns as members of the family. It took above-average strength and a steady eye to hold and aim this sixty-four-inch, twelve-pound rifle. When it was packed with extra powder, Daniel Boone's Tick Licker was known to score bull's-eyes at four hundred yards. Less certain is the legend that says Boone once shot a tick off a bear's snout at a hundred yards.

The Wilderness Road was not the only route open to easterners eager to settle in Kentucky. Many pioneers chose to float down the Ohio River. Most stepped ashore at Limestone (now Maysville), Kentucky. In one seven-month stretch in 1786–87, 177 heavily loaded flatboats passed a riverside army post.

A NEW LIFE BEYOND THE MOUNTAINS

According to army records, the boats carried 2,689 people, 1,333 horses, 786 cattle, and 102 wagons.[1]

River pilots had to cope with shifting sandbars, tricky currents, snags, rocks, and other dangers. Boats that smashed into hidden obstructions often broke apart or capsized. A far greater threat, however, came from the American Indians who roamed the banks of the river. Enraged at the threat to their hunting grounds, the nearby tribes declared war on river traffic.

Boats that stayed well out in the current usually passed beyond the range of arrows and musket fire. To counter this tactic, the American Indians did their best to lure the boats close to shore. In 1790, one flatboat pilot took the bait—two "white men" who ran along the bank, pleading for help. As the boat drew closer, a volley of Shawnee rifle fire killed two of the six people aboard. The survivors surrendered, and then watched in horror as the raiders scalped their dead friends. After drinking a keg of whiskey from the boat's stores, the Shawnee burned one captive at the stake. A second man was forced to run the gauntlet (a double line of warriors armed with clubs and sticks). Weeks later, the tribe ransomed a third captive for six hundred silver brooches.[2]

Down on the Tennessee River, a tribe of Chickamagua Indians paid dearly for staging a similar

River travel exposed settlers to dangers that ranged from tricky currents to attacks by American Indians. In this 1868 engraving, the current has swept a flatboat close to shore, giving a raiding party a chance to spring a trap.

attack. Spotting a flatboat lagging far behind its companions, warriors pursued it in their canoes. After fighting their way aboard they killed the men and carried off the women and children as captives. What the Chickamagua did not know was that several of their captives were ill with smallpox. Before long the disease was spreading through nearby villages. As the epidemic raged, raids on the Cumberland River settlements almost ceased. By the time the disease ran its course, the settlements had grown strong enough to defend themselves.

Housing a Pioneer Family

In the periods of peace between American Indian uprisings, frontier settlers had little time for leisure. Turning wooded, brush-covered tracts of land into productive farms required endless hours of hard work. There were cabins to build, land to clear, animals to tend, and crops to plant. Each family had to contend with bad weather, crop failures, and the loneliness of life on the frontier.

Daniel Drake grew up on a frontier farm and went on to become a well-loved doctor and teacher. He was only three years old when his father, Isaac Drake, loaded the family onto a flatboat and floated down the Ohio River in 1788. The journey ended near Washington, in northeastern Kentucky. There Isaac and four friends bought 1,400 acres of woodland. Because Isaac Drake had little cash, his family's share came to only thirty-eight acres.

Late in life, Drake wrote long letters in which he described those early years. The family's first task was to build a shelter—a windowless, one-story log cabin. When they moved in, the wooden chimney and shingled roof were only half finished. Walking across the dirt floor meant stepping from sleeper to sleeper. Sleepers were poles the settlers put down to support the roughly dressed floor timbers (puncheons) they would add later. Although the cabin was crude, even by frontier standards, the family rejoiced in its new home. Drake later recalled the sight of "two children—a brother & sister—sitting on the ground between [the sleepers], as joyous as you ever saw."[3]

Over the next six years, Isaac Drake slowly improved the cabin. He added the missing section of roof, the puncheon floor, a small window, and a chimney made of small poles held together by mortar. The family's rifle, vital for both hunting and defense, was hung close to hand on pegs driven into the log wall. The Drakes also kept their axe under the bed at night, ready in case of trouble. Each morning, someone climbed to the loft and peered through the cracks between the logs. If no danger lurked outside, the lookout called that it was safe to open the door. This dread of an American Indian ambush hovered over every cabin in the region. Mothers shushed noisy children by telling them, "Lie still and go to sleep, or the Shawnees will catch you."[4]

In time, scattered clusters of cabins grew into settlements. Long before he became president, Theodore

Roosevelt wrote about these "rude, straggling, unkempt villages." A typical settlement, he said, contained a store or two, a tavern where travelers were devoured by fleas, a log schoolhouse, and a small church.[5] In the deeper woods, families worked together to build small forts known as stations. Each was guarded by a stout stockade made of logs. The backs of a row of cabins formed one wall, and a blockhouse stood at each corner. Loopholes cut in the walls gave riflemen a clear field of fire. When danger threatened, men raced to lower the crossbar that secured the heavy gate. The fort was a welcome refuge during times of danger, but settlers counted the days spent there as days wasted. Their lives were centered on their clearings—the farms they were carving out of the wilderness.

Putting Food on the Table

Pioneer families depended on four food sources: the crops they raised, the livestock they tended, the nuts and berries they gathered, and the wild game they hunted. In the early months, game was so plentiful that people tired of eating turkey, buffalo, deer, and bear. Drake remembered wild turkeys so fat that when they fell after being shot, "their skins would burst."[6] The days of easy hunting ended all too quickly. Daniel Boone complained of the "great waste in killing meat. Some would kill three, four, five or one-half dozen buffaloes and not take half a horse load from them all." Within six weeks of arriving at Boonesborough, he said, hunters were being forced to travel fifteen or twenty miles to find game.[7]

Once the backbreaking toil of cutting trees and clearing brush was finished, the rich Kentucky soil produced bumper harvests. Farmers relied on Indian corn to feed their families and their animals—cows, horses, hogs, sheep, and even dogs. Men headed out on a long hunt carried dried corn in their pouches as emergency rations. Once the fields were cleared and plowed, a cornfield could produce sixty to eighty bushels per acre. The greatest dangers to the growing corn were crows, squirrels, and bad weather. The children armed

In times of trouble Kentucky's pioneer families gathered at strongpoints such as Boonesborough. Once the gates swung shut, riflemen stood guard in the two-story blockhouses.

themselves with sticks, stones, and even shotguns to scare away hungry pests. Nothing, however, could save the crop if an untimely frost nipped the ripening ears. The payoff was in the eating. "My first business in the morning," Drake recalls, "was to pull, and husk and silk enough [ears] for breakfast. [When] eaten with new milk, what breakfast could be more delicious?"[8]

Each farmer set aside a small plot for a truck garden. These gardens produced crops that added variety to the diet—melons, turnips, squash, beans, and pumpkins. The sight of huge, orange pumpkins growing in the garden was cause for rejoicing. Families ate pumpkin in pies and boiled the flesh to make molasses. Cows fed on pumpkin were said to produce milk that was rich and sweet. During the winter, dried pumpkin was a favorite treat. Children also looked forward to nights spent in front of a hickory fire, scraping and eating juicy turnips. The turnips were so tasty, Drake said, that older settlers no longer hungered for the apples and pears of their youth.[9]

The pioneer era passed quickly. As settlements turned into towns and the roads improved, general stores opened their doors. Storekeepers did a brisk trade in goods that the settlers could not make or grow. Farmers bartered furs and deerskins for coffee, rum, gunpowder, plows, shoes, and petticoats. Offered tea for the first time, some tried to eat the leaves with butter and salt. As their farms grew in size, farmers planted cash crops—hemp, tobacco, and wheat. Small factories and mills sprang up to turn hemp into rope, tobacco into cigars, and wheat into flour. In 1812, breeders shipped half a million hogs eastward via the Kaintuck Hog Road, a route that followed the old Wilderness Road into Virginia. By then two products destined to make Kentucky famous also were heading for market—whiskey and fine horses.

"Half Horse, Half Alligator"

The tough Kentucky boatmen who sailed down the Mississippi claimed to be "half horse and half alligator."[11] When challenged, they backed up their boast with fists, knives, and guns. Like all Kentuckians, these men were fiercely independent. At the same time, they knew that a settlement would thrive only if neighbor helped neighbor. New settlers could count on the community for help with house-raisings. Entire families turned out for corn-shuckings, log-rollings, and house-warmings. When the work was done, the hosts served feasts of venison, melons, apple pies, bowls of milk, and pitchers of cider. Only the old folks kept their seats when a guest struck up a tune on the fiddle and the dancing started.

Young men tried to impress the girls by showing off. They wrestled, raced horses, and lifted flour barrels above their heads. At corn-shuckings, two teams raced to see who could strip the cornhusks the fastest. As the work progressed and the whiskey jug made the rounds, the joking and boasting grew louder. "It was there," Drake writes, "that I first learned that competition is the mother of cheating, falsehood and broils [brawls]."[12]

NOT A SOUL WAS THEN SETTLED ON THE OHIO BETWEEN WHEELING AND LOUISVILLE, A SPACE OF FIVE HUNDRED OR SIX HUNDRED MILES. . . . [T]HOUGH IT WAS NOW WINTER, NOT A SOUL IN ALL BEARGRASS SETTLEMENT WAS IN SAFETY BUT BY BEING IN A FORT. I THEN MEDITATED TRAVELING ABOUT EIGHTY MILES TO CRAIG'S STATION, ON GILBERT'S CREEK, IN LINCOLN COUNTY. WE SET OUT IN A FEW DAYS; NEARLY ALL I OWNED WAS THEN AT STAKE. I HAD THREE HORSES, TWO OF THEM WERE PACKED, THE OTHER MY WIFE RODE, WITH AS MUCH LUMBER AS THE BEAST COULD BEAR. . . . THE PACK HORSES WERE LED, ONE BY MYSELF, THE OTHER BY MY MAN. THE TRACE [PATH], WHAT THERE WAS BEING SO NARROW AND BAD, WE HAD NO CHANCE BUT TO WADE THROUGH ALL THE MUD, RIVERS, AND CREEKS WE CAME TO. SALT RIVER, WITH A NUMBER OF ITS LARGE BRANCHES, WE HAD TO DEAL WITH OFTEN; THOSE WATERS BEING FLUSH, WE OFTEN MUST WADE TO OUR MIDDLE. . . . THOSE STRUGGLES OFTEN MADE US FORGET THE DANGERS WE HAD FROM INDIANS. . . . AFTER SIX DAYS PAINFUL TRAVEL OF THIS KIND, WE ARRIVED AT CRAIG'S STATION A LITTLE BEFORE CHRISTMAS, AND ABOUT THREE MONTHS AFTER OUR START FROM VIRGINIA.[10]

Samuel Taylor kept this matter-of-fact record of his journey from Virginia to Kentucky in 1783. Like almost all of his fellow pioneers, he accepted the trip's dangers and hardships without complaint. Unlike many settlers, he chose to follow the Ohio River into Kentucky instead of taking the more popular Wilderness Road.

A well-stocked pioneer cabin held everything a family needed to survive on the frontier. In this crowded corner, tobacco leaves are drying, tools hang at the ready, and a bearskin pays tribute to the hunting skills of the family's menfolk.

As the evening wore on and tempers grew short, fights often broke out. The combatants hit, kicked, gouged, and bit as the other men cheered them on. The fight did not end until the loser hollered "Enough!" That was a signal for the victor to crow and flap his arms as he danced a rowdy jig.[13]

A backwoods wedding was an equally lively affair. The bridegroom and his friends began the day by riding at breakneck speed to the bride's home. As the day wore on, the guests gathered to inspect her dowry. Most girls started marriage with a brood mare, a cow, a bed and bedding, and a trunk filled with clothes. When all was ready, the couple knelt before a preacher to say their vows. After the bride's mother served a wedding feast, the fiddlers struck up a lively tune, and the dancing started.

As the candles burned low, the unmarried young women took the bride up to the loft to prepare her for bed. That was the signal for the young men to loudly advise the groom on his marriage duties. A final round of toasts wished the couple joy and a house full of healthy children. Later everyone would gather to build a cabin for the newlyweds.[14] With the support of the community behind them, the marriage was off to a good start.

★ EVEN THE KIDS HAD WORK TO DO ★

Pioneer parents believed that "the Devil finds work for idle hands." If that was true, pioneer children had little time for mischief. There was a mountain of work to do, and each child was expected to do his or her share. Modern children might be surprised to learn that their distant cousins seldom protested the seemingly endless chores. Pioneer children understood that the family's survival depended on getting the work done.

Daniel Drake never forgot the tasks he performed on the family's backwoods farm. As a twelve-year-old, he carried water from the spring, grated corn for cornmeal, and kept the calf quiet while his mother, Elizabeth, milked the cow. In December he helped his father, Isaac, butcher hogs so that the family could eat bacon, sausages, and mince pies. He also chopped wood for the fire, fed and

Neighbors pitch in to help newcomers build the cabin that will shelter them during the coming winter.

tended the horses, helped with the soapmaking, and churned the butter. That long, dull process was not his favorite chore. "If I could have as many . . . wishes gratified as I uttered wishes that the butter 'would come,'" Drake wrote, "I should have nothing *more* to wish for in this life."[15]

Like most boys, Daniel preferred to work in the fields. The soil was so full of roots that it took a father-son team to do the plowing. While his father handled the plow, Daniel sat astride the horse and kept it plodding forward. While riding bareback on a "lean and lazy horse" for hours at a time, he sometimes daydreamed. Each time his mind drifted, it seemed, the plow would hit a tough, thick root. Then, as the horse jerked to a stop, young Daniel would be thrown against the horse's collar. He later described the shock as "a hard and unlooked for punch in the pit of the stomach."[16]

Even a simple chore sometimes went awry. When Daniel was six, his mother sent him to borrow some salt from a neighbor. This was no small errand, for salt was so precious it sold for three dollars a bushel. The neighbor tied the salt in a piece of paper, and Daniel set out on his return journey. When he was halfway home the paper tore, and most of the salt spilled on the ground. A tearful Daniel ran home to report the loss, certain he was due for a whipping. In the Drake household, as he knew all too well, wasting food was a major sin. Luckily for Daniel, Elizabeth Drake did not blame him for the loss. The paper, she judged, had not been properly tied.[17]

6

KENTUCKY COMES OF AGE

If Richard Henderson had fulfilled his dream, today's maps would say Transylvania instead of Kentucky. The fact that he failed was not for lack of effort. After reaching Boonesborough on April 20, 1775, the lawyer did everything in his power to separate the territory from Virginia.

Henderson first drew up some plans to turn Boonesborough into a safe and sturdy fortress. Daniel Boone tried to get the work started, but had trouble rounding up workers. The men told him they were busy staking out claims and putting in crops. As one visitor noted, "You could not discover what person commanded, for in fact no person did actually command anything."[1] As the confusion mounted, Henderson called on the settlers to attend an assembly. Men rode in from Harrodsburg, Logan's Station, and Boiling Spring to discuss the future.

The assembly met under a huge elm tree on May 24. Henderson told the men it was their job to bring justice and freedom to the colony. The settlers could write their own laws, he said—but his company retained the right to veto them.[2] After some heated debate, the men agreed on a court system and a militia. Next the assembly passed laws against swearing and breaking the Sabbath. That was when Boone pushed through two measures of his own. One warned hunters not to kill more game than they could use. The second called for the breeding of fine horses.

Henderson's dreams of owning his own colony quickly ran into major roadblocks. Virginia and North Carolina stoutly refused to recognize his deal with the Cherokee. Virginia, in particular, saw little reason to give up its claims to Kentucky. That feeling grew stronger when the Revolution broke out in 1776. No one had time to worry about a dream called Transylvania while there were Redcoats to fight. In December, the assembly cut deeper into Henderson's plans by making Kentucky a full-fledged Virginia county. To pay off the Transylvania Company's claims, the colonial assembly awarded Henderson and his partners the rights to two hundred thousand acres near the Green River in northwestern Kentucky. The city of Henderson took root there, a lasting reminder of the role the Transylvania Company had played in settling the territory.

Even as Virginia was chipping away at his plans, Henderson was losing support in Kentucky. When his company doubled the price of land, the settlers argued that it had broken the promises that brought them across the mountains. The feud with the Transylvania Company was soon forgotten, however. Women and children were arriving to join their husbands and fathers. His wife and daughters, Boone said proudly, were the first white women to settle in Kentucky.

With the British urging them on, the Mingo, Wyandot, and Shawnee tribes went on the warpath. Warriors launched attacks on Boonesborough and the other frontier forts. A few small settlements fell, but the rest of the settlers holed up in their strongholds and held on. After the long war dragged to a close, the trickle of settlers turned into a torrent. Towns and villages sprang up along the Wilderness Road. Danville, Frankfort, Lexington, and Louisville grew in importance. The new era brought progress, but it also clogged the courts with cases involving faulty land titles.

Muddled Land Claims

After the Revolutionary War ended in 1781, more and more families poured into the "land of tomorrow." With them came speculators intent on picking up unclaimed land they could sell for big profits. Virginia added to the confusion by paying soldiers with warrants that promised their holders up to five thousand acres of land in Kentucky County. Anxious to cash in their certificates, the veterans joined the speculators in a race to stake their claims.

The surveyors who laid out property lines were mostly untrained hunters and farmers. Most, like Daniel Boone, worked in good faith. The poorly defined boundaries they laid out, however, produced a

As early as 1796, wagons began moving freely over the newly widened Wilderness Road. When this photo was taken nearly a hundred years later, little had changed. It would be another twenty years before builders would arrive to lay blacktop over the muddy ruts of the old roadbed.

crazy quilt of overlapping tracts. One of Boone's early surveys began at "two Hickories and a White Oak being Madison's SE Corner, Thence East 92 Poles [one pole equals 16.5 feet] to a White Oak, Thence S 25 E 118 Poles to Two Ciders on Bogses Fork, Thence East 88 Poles . . ." and so on, back "to the Beginning."[3] It was not long before a clever lawyer raised the obvious question: Which white oaks did Boone mean, out of the hundreds found in those woods?

Judges worked overtime as claims and counter-claims piled up. As a rule, the victories went to the rich, who knew how to twist the law to suit their needs. Many small farmers lost their land, or saw their holdings reduced. A few unlucky families were reduced to renting land they had once farmed as their own. Boone, who thought he owned thousands of acres, saw his claims slowly whittled away. He held on for a time, and then fled to friendlier fields. One writer summed up the results of this legal thievery in these words: "Kentucky became a place of landlords and tenants, of rich estates for the few and second- or third-rate smaller farms for the many."[4]

Kentucky Joins the Union

Even as they sorted out muddled land claims, Kentuckians chafed under Virginia's heavy hand. The assembly in Richmond, they complained, did little to defend them from American Indian raids. As months passed, the feeling grew that Kentucky should break its ties to Virginia. The problem lay in writing a constitution that all could support. One radical group spoke of forming an independent nation allied to Spain. A larger group wanted to join the Union. For eight long years, conventions met and argued. Some of the more heated debates ended in fistfights, and a few led to duels. The climax came in 1792, when delegates at last signed off on a constitution. On June 1 of that year, the United States welcomed Kentucky as the fifteenth state.

The new constitution looked both forward and backward. On the plus side, free white adult males were given the vote, whether or not they owned land. The practice of throwing debtors into prison was abolished. Voice voting gave way to the secret ballot. On the minus side, the governor and state senators were chosen by electors, not by direct vote of the people. In 1799 county courts were given the power to tax and regulate business. That was a further blow to democracy because in that era "men of property" controlled the courts. By the mid-1800s, one observer noted, county offices were "sold like a horse in the public market so that he who had the most money might get the office."[5]

A New Kind of Hero

Kentucky's growing pains failed to slow traffic on the Wilderness Road. The promise of cheap land and elbow room drew more and more people westward. The newcomers told tall tales around their campfires of what it meant to be a Kentuckian. Bears "can't stand Kentucky play," James Finley wrote, "[because] biting and gouging are too hard for them."[7] As the wilderness retreated, a new kind of leader emerged. One of the best known was a scoundrel named James Wilkinson.

Wilkinson arrived on the Kentucky scene in 1785. A native of Maryland, he had climbed to the rank of brigadier general during the Revolution. The tall, smooth-talking newcomer promptly built a thriving trade in salt and hides. A taste for high living, however, kept him in debt. The solution, he reasoned, lay in

DURING MY BOYHOOD, THERE WAS IN THE COUNTRY . . . A GREAT DEFICIENCY OF BOOKS. THERE WAS NOT A SINGLE BOOK STORE NORTH OF LICKING RIVER AND, PERHAPS, NONE IN THE STATE. ALL THE BOOKS IMPORTED WERE KEPT IN WHAT WERE CALLED *STORES*, . . . VARIETY SHOPS, IF NOT CURIOSITY SHOPS—COMPREHENDING DRY GOODS, HARDWARE, GLASS & EARTHEN WARE, GROCERIES, DYESTUFFS & DRUGS, AMMUNITION, HATS, MANUFACTURES OF LEATHER, BOOKS, AND STATIONERY—THE LAST CONSISTING GENERALLY OF COARSE FOOLS CAP, WAFERS, SLATES & PENCILS. . . .

OF OUR OWN LIBRARY I HAVE ALREADY SPOKEN INCIDENTALLY. A FAMILY BIBLE, RIPPON'S HYMNS, WATTS' HYMNS FOR CHILDREN, THE PILGRIMS PROGRESS, AN OLD ROMANCE OF THE DAYS OF KNIGHT ERRANTRY, PRIMERS, . . . SPELLING BOOKS, AN ARITHMETIC & A NEW ALMANAC FOR THE NEW YEAR, COMPOSED ALL THAT I CAN RECOLLECT, TILL WITHIN 2 OR 3 YEARS OF MY LEAVING HOME.[6]

Late in his life, Daniel Drake looked back fondly at the years he spent growing up on a wilderness farm. In this letter to "my dear Dove," his oldest daughter, he describes the range of goods sold in the general store in the nearby village. If more books had been available, he writes, "it is probable that I should have made some proficiency by solitary study at night and on rainy days."

Progress came swiftly to Harrodsburg and other Kentucky towns after the Revolutionary War. A pioneer builder named Joseph Morgan put up these handsome row houses in 1807. The tavern that once did business here reigned as the center of Harrodsburg's lively social life.

opening new markets for Kentucky's products. The pack trains that traveled eastward on the Wilderness Road moved too slowly. If only the Spanish would open the Mississippi River to American shippers! With that goal in mind, Wilkinson loaded two flatboats with tobacco and floated down to New Orleans. When he returned a year later, he brought good news. The Spanish governor, he said, had agreed to open the port.

As time passed, the details of Wilkinson's secret pact with the Spanish came to light. Only one trade permit had been issued—and it belonged to James Wilkinson. Anyone else who wanted to ship goods through New Orleans had to deal with him. To win this prize (and a yearly payment in gold), Wilkinson had promised to push Kentucky toward independence. To speed up the process, he planned to use Spanish gold to bribe those who opposed his plan. If a

As the pioneer era passed into history, Kentucky's farmers turned to producing cash crops for eastern markets. This farmer proudly displays his tobacco barn, where he'll tend the valuable leaves as they dry.

peaceful approach failed, he would mount a rebellion, using guns furnished by the Spanish. Once free of its ties to Virginia, he promised, the fledgling republic would ally itself with Spain. Wilkinson, as a matter of course, reserved the future governor's chair for himself.

In the end Spain's investment brought little return. Wilkinson pushed hard for independence at the convention of 1788, but was voted down. When they saw that the plan had stalled, the Spanish opened New Orleans to all shippers. With his grand design in tatters, Wilkinson left Kentucky and rejoined the U.S. Army. Because no one knew of his ties to Spain, he was allowed to assume his old rank. By 1796 he had risen to the rank of commanding general.

In 1805, President Thomas Jefferson picked the wily Wilkinson to serve as governor of the newly purchased Louisiana Territory.

James Wilkinson was a wildly ambitious soldier and businessman. In return for the right to ship goods through New Orleans, Wilkinson secretly promised the Spanish that he would help add Kentucky to the Spanish empire. The scheme eventually fell through.

After taking up his new job he received a visit from Aaron Burr, the former vice president. Burr promptly enlisted Wilkinson in a traitorous plan designed to annex Louisiana and the Southwest as an independent country. Wilkinson worked with Burr for a time, but then had a change of heart. In a letter to the president, Wilkinson denounced Burr's "deep, dark, wicked, and widespread conspiracy." Burr tried to tie his fellow traitor to the plot, but he could not prove his charges.

Wilkinson survived the scandal and went on to fight in the War of 1812. His career ended after he bungled the campaign against Montreal. By the time he died in Mexico in 1825, Kentuckians were too busy to mourn a former hero. The era of the Wilderness Road was drawing to a close.

★ DANIEL BOONE: THE FINAL YEARS ★

As the country filled up behind him, Daniel Boone kept moving westward. After leaving Boonesborough he settled on the far side of the Kentucky River at Boone Station. There he raised tobacco, ran surveys for newcomers, and enjoyed the fine hunting. When neighbors crowded in too close, he moved to Limestone and opened a store and a tavern. As usual, Rebecca did most of the routine daily chores. Her footloose husband hunted and ran surveys for new settlers.

Unlike James Wilkinson, Boone had no desire to live in a fine house and wear silk shirts. He was content if he could provide for his family and live where there was good hunting. Like his fellow pioneers, he thought himself rich if he owned a fertile piece of land. To that end,

DURING THE FIRST PERIOD OF [KENTUCKY'S] SETTLEMENT, ... THE TABLE WAS ENTIRELY FURNISHED WITH THE PRODUCE OF THE COUNTRY; AND VERY FEW ARTICLES OF CLOTHING, OR OF WOOLLEN OR LINEN FOR DOMESTIC USE, WERE BROUGHT FROM ANY OTHER COUNTRY. . . . BUT AS SOON AS GREAT SUMS OF MONEY WERE INTRODUCED, . . . A CHANGE TOOK PLACE IN OUR MANNERS. . . .

HOME MANUFACTURES WERE NOT ONLY DISCARDED FROM OUR DRESS BUT WERE ALSO LAID ASIDE IN OUR DIET. NONE BUT IMPORTED CHEESE WAS FIT TO BE SERVED UPON A GENTEEL TABLE; COUNTRY SUGAR DID NOT AGREE WITH THEIR STOMACHS; AND . . . WINE AND IMPORTED SPIRITS WERE USED AS FREELY AS IF THEY FLOWED SPONTANEOUSLY FROM OUR SPRINGS. NOT SATISFIED WITH THESE ALTERNATIONS THEY TURNED DAY INTO NIGHT, AND NIGHT INTO DAY, AND EVERY EXPENSIVE AND RIDICULOUS FASHION WHICH WAS IN USE IN ANY OF THE OLD COUNTRIES WAS INTRODUCED HERE.

—THE *KENTUCKY HERALD*, 1797[9]

The pioneer lifestyle retreated to Kentucky's remote valleys after good times arrived in the late 1780s. In the fast-growing towns, drafty log cabins gave way to fine brick houses. Shop owners stocked their shelves with imported goods such as tea, nutmeg, satin waistcoats, and Scottish snuff. When hard times returned in 1797, the Kentucky Herald *blamed the "change in the manners" of the people for the turnaround.*

Boone surveyed and claimed thousands of acres. Because he was a woodsman and not a lawyer, he often failed to complete the paperwork. That oversight cost him dearly as the years marched past.

Like all frontier regions, Kentucky attracted a fair share of shady characters. When a claim-jumper spotted a flaw in one of Boone's claims, he quietly filed legal papers that challenged the woodsman's title. As one lawsuit followed another, Boone lost most of his hard-won land. To make matters worse, the state auctioned off more of his acres because he could not pay his taxes.

Boone was almost sixty years old when Kentucky became a state in 1792. His eyes were keen, but his joints ached. He still hunted, but often took Rebecca along to keep camp. He was living at Brushy Fork when his son Daniel, Jr., told him about a new frontier out in Missouri. To entice the famous American, the Spanish governor offered him 850 acres if he would move there. Boone gathered up his family and walked the seven hundred miles to his new home on the Missouri River.

The old woodsman made his last long hunt in 1810. He felt almost young again, hunting and trapping along the Yellowstone River in Wyoming. Rebecca died three years later, at age seventy-four. To compound his grief, Boone had to sell his Missouri land to pay off his creditors. "I have paid all my debts," he declared. "No one will say when I am gone, 'Boone was a dishonest man.'"[8]

Before he died in 1820 Daniel Boone often spoke of himself as a "common man." All who knew him thought otherwise. The pioneer who built the Wilderness Road was a most uncommon man.

The population num-
bers tell the tale. In
1800, twenty-five years
after Daniel Boone

END OF
AN ERA

opened the Wilderness
Road, 221,000 people
were living in Kentucky.
Ten years later that num-
ber had nearly doubled,
to 407,000. By this time
Tennessee was filling up
as well. In 1820, a tenth of the nation's 10 million
people were living in Kentucky and Tennessee.
America was on the move, and the movement was ever
westward.[1]

Some of the new settlers were farm families from
the east, drawn by tales of fertile soil and forests teem-
ing with game. Adding to the westbound stream were
immigrants newly arrived from Ireland, Germany, and
England. More than five hundred thousand Europeans
flooded into the United States between 1830 and
1840. A fair number settled on the Atlantic coast, but
many headed west where land was cheap. The government was selling land, good or bad, for a rock-bottom
price of $1.25 an acre. In 1836, sales soared to over 20
million acres.[2] As soon as one region filled up, settlers
spilled over into another . . . and another.

The Shakers lived in communal houses near Harrodsburg and were among the most successful of Kentucky's settlers. Today, volunteers keep the homes and meeting hall open for tourists who wish to sample the crafts, music, and food of these peaceful and industrious pioneers.

In the 1790s some Kentucky towns died and others flourished. Boonesborough dwindled to a tiny hamlet, and the old fort fell into decay. Lexington, by contrast, blossomed as a cultural and business center. In 1800 the population stood at 1,806 people, including 439 slaves. Farmers drove wagons loaded with hemp, wheat, and tobacco down Main Street. A university was in the works, and a fine new courthouse stood atop Mars Hill. Traffic still moved on the old Wilderness Road, but the frontier was moving westward.

Twilight of the Wilderness Road

The Wilderness Road never inspired travelers to sing its praises. One writer described it as full of "mud and holes, and jutting ledges of rock and loose boulders, and twists and turns, and general total depravity."[3] At night, migrants huddled around tiny fires as the women dished out the family's meager rations. Babies cried and children shivered as wind, rain, and hail whipped through the trees. Only the vision of fertile bluegrass meadows kept the settlers trudging onward.

Over the years work crews improved a few stretches of the Wilderness Road. Settlers, however, still had no choice but to leave their wagons behind when they reached the Cumberland Gap. Isaac Shelby, Kentucky's first governor, vowed to change all that. In 1795 he pushed a bill through the legislature that budgeted 2,000 English pounds for his pet project. Once it was widened to thirty feet, Shelby promised, the Wilderness Road would carry wagons loaded with up to a ton of cargo.

Daniel Boone saw the plan as a chance to make some much-needed cash. After all, he reasoned, he had never been paid for his work on the original Wilderness Road. The collapse of the Transylvania Company had left Boone with nothing but land claims, and the courts had stolen those. Besides, Boone knew Shelby from the old days at Boonesborough. He picked up a quill pen and wrote this letter (printed here with his highly original spelling and punctuation):

Feburey the 11th 1796

Sir

    after my best Respts to your Excelancy and famyly I wish to inform you that I have sum intention of undertaking this New Rode that is to be cut through the Wilderness and I think my Self intitled to the ofer of the Bisness as I first Marked out that Rode in March 1775 and never rec'd anything for my trubel and Sepose I am No Statesman I am a Woodsman and think My Self as Capable of Marking and Cutting that Rode as any other man. Sir if you think with Me I would thank you to wright me a Line by the post the first oportuneaty and he Will Lodge it at Mr. John Miler son hinkston fork as I wish to know Where and When it is to be Laat So that I may atend at the time,

    I am Deer Sir your very omble Sarvent.

DANIEL BOONE[4]

The letter may have touched Shelby's heart, but it came too late. The Wilderness Road contract was already signed. James Knox and Joseph Crockett put a team of surveyors and builders to work in the summer of 1796. By October the new and improved road was carrying traffic over the hundred miles from Cumberland Gap to Crab Orchard. The *Kentucky Gazette* featured the road opening on its front page:

THE WILDERNESS ROAD from Cumberland Gap to the settlements in Kentucky is now compleated. Waggons loaded with a ton weight, may pass with ease, with four good horses. Travellers will find no difficulty in procuring such necessaries as they stand in need of on the road; and the abundant crop now growing in Kentucky, will afford the emigrants a certainty of being supplied with every necessary of life on the most convenient terms.[5]

For a time traffic flowed more smoothly on the new road. Constant use, however, soon ruined the roadbed. Axles snapped and loads spilled when wagons hit a pothole or slid down a steep, muddy grade. Drivers cursed as they struggled to keep their rigs from being swept away while fording rivers and streams. Everyone knew that bridges were badly needed, but lawmakers refused to spend tax money for improvements. Instead, they copied an eastern custom and allowed private citizens to build toll roads. Tollgates soon dotted the landscape, slowing traffic and raising tempers. Travelers and shippers fought back by seeking faster, cheaper routes. By 1840 the Wilderness Road was almost forgotten.

Westbound Traffic Shifts to Two Northern Roads

As Boone's old road fell into disuse, overland traffic shifted to the Pennsylvania Road and the National Road. The Pennsylvania Road, one of the young nation's few gravel roads, was finished in 1796. The route began at Philadelphia, wound westward through the mountains, and ended at the bustling river port of Pittsburgh. The city stood at the natural crossroads where the Allegheny and Monongahela Rivers meet to form the mighty Ohio. From Pittsburgh, travelers sailed down the Ohio River to Kentucky, Ohio, and points west. The coming of the railroads and the opening of the Pennsylvania Canal robbed the road of its importance in the mid-1800s. Today, drivers who speed along

As the demand for lumber grew, wagons loaded with steam-powered sawmill equipment clattered over the Wilderness Road. Soon the powerful sawblades were turning out the lumber needed to build Lexington, Louisville, and other Kentucky cities.

U.S. 30 are following the route of the old Pennsylvania Road.

The National Road (also called the Cumberland Road) was America's first interstate highway.[6] The initial section of the heavily traveled road ran from Cumberland, Maryland, to Wheeling, West Virginia. From Wheeling the road headed west to meet the Mississippi River at St. Louis. Thirty feet wide with an eighty-foot right-of-way, the first section was finished in 1818. The sections beyond Wheeling took longer to complete—the road did not reach Columbus, Ohio, until 1833. Some twenty-five years later it crept into Vandalia, Illinois.

The National Road was one of the marvels of its age. Onlookers admired the smooth roadway and its "numerous and stately stone bridges, . . . its iron mile-posts, and its old iron gates." To speed travelers on their way, relays of fresh horses were stationed every twelve miles or so. Teams were changed "almost in the twinkling of an eye. . . . The moment the team came to a halt the driver threw down the reins and almost instantly the incoming team was detached, a fresh one attached, the reins thrown back to the driver, . . . and away again went the coach at full speed."[7]

Observers counted as many as twenty coaches and heavy freight wagons lined up at one time. The coaches ran both day and night. People who lived nearby said they could tell time by their coming and going. Farmers added to the gridlock by herding horses, mules, cattle, hogs, and sheep along the right-of-way. After long-distance traffic fell off in the 1850s, the road survived to serve local towns and farmers. Today, U.S. 40 retraces the route once honored as America's National Road.

Cruisin' Down the O-hi-o

The U.S. Army took charge of frontier defenses in 1816. Troops stationed at forts along the Mississippi and Arkansas Rivers protected settlers from American Indian raids. The government also pressured tribes

OLD AMERICA SEEMS TO BE BREAKING UP AND MOVING WESTWARD. WE ARE SELDOM OUT OF SIGHT, AS WE TRAVEL ON THIS GRAND TRACK TOWARDS THE OHIO, OF FAMILY GROUPS, BEHIND AND BEFORE US, SOME WITH A VIEW TO A PARTICULAR SPOT; CLOSE TO A BROTHER, PERHAPS, OR A FRIEND, WHO HAS GONE BEFORE, AND REPORTED WELL OF THE COUNTRY. MANY, LIKE OURSELVES, WHEN THEY ARRIVE IN THE WILDERNESS, WILL FIND NO LODGE PREPARED FOR THEM.

A SMALL WAGON (SO LIGHT THAT YOU MIGHT ALMOST CARRY IT, YET STRONG ENOUGH TO BEAR A GOOD LOAD OF BEDDING, UTENSILS, AND PROVISIONS, AND A SWARM OF YOUNG CITIZENS,—AND TO SUSTAIN MARVELLOUS SHOCKS IN ITS PASSAGE OVER THESE ROCKY HEIGHTS), WITH TWO SMALL HORSES; SOMETIMES A COW OR TWO, COMPRISES THEIR ALL; EXCEPTING A LITTLE STORE OF HARD-EARNED CASH FOR THE LAND OFFICE OF THE DISTRICT; WHERE THEY MAY OBTAIN A TITLE FOR AS MANY ACRES AS THEY POSSESS HALF-DOLLARS, BEING ONE-FOURTH OF THE PURCHASE MONEY.[8]

By 1818 the National Road (also known as the Cumberland Road) was carrying a steady stream of settlers into the western territories. Kentucky was filling up, and newcomers were attracted to the wilderness north of the Ohio River. Morris Birkbeck, an English immigrant, wrote this description of the traffic he met on his journey westward.

living east of the Mississippi to exchange their lands for cash payments and gifts. Once the treaties were signed, the tribes moved to new homes farther west. Settlers followed hard on their heels, eager to claim new homesteads.

River travel, without American Indians lying in ambush, cut weeks from the westward journey. Some settlers built and sailed their own flatboats downriver. Others loaded their household goods and livestock onto the swifter keelboats. River craft began to make regular trips between Pittsburgh and Louisville, and between Louisville and New Orleans. In 1807, for example, New Orleans recorded the arrival of 755 "barges and flats." By 1813 the number had almost doubled to 1,306.[9]

The simplest river craft was the raft. A young Abraham Lincoln was one of the rafters who floated downriver, delivered cargo, and sold the rafts to be cut into lumber. Families sometimes made their own rafts and poled them downstream. When they reached their destination, the sale of the raft and its timbers helped pay for a wagon or some cattle. The flatboat was a step up in comfort. These flat-bottomed craft were twelve or fourteen feet wide and up to fifty feet long. The gunwales (sides) supported a roof that ran the length of the flatboat. The bow was raked forward to cut smoothly through the water. Most flatboats carried a crew of three, as well as a cargo of forty to fifty tons. Some were equipped with sails and boasted of brick chimneys.

Road-builders completed the first major widening of the Wilderness Road in 1796. In time, potholes and slippery grades gave way to smooth-surfaced roadbeds. Today, well-hidden from busy Interstates, the old road still carries local traffic through the peaceful Virginia and Kentucky countryside.

Builders soon took the basic flatboat design and added rounded bottoms, keels, and pointed bows. Lighter, faster, and easier to steer, keelboats became the elite river craft of their day. They sailed well in shallow waters and carried cargoes of up to fifty tons. Like the flatboats, the decks were roofed, and a square sail could be unfurled when the winds were right. A keelboat crew consisted of a captain and as many as twelve oarsmen. Propelled by both wind and oars, flatboats and keelboats could be sailed upriver as well as down.

The flatboats and keelboats favored by early settlers fell into disfavor when steamboats reached the Ohio and Missouri Rivers. In this 1878 engraving, workmen are shaping the hull of a new stern-wheel steamboat (far right.)

River travel exposed boatmen and passengers to an abundance of dangers. Storms, sandbars, fast currents, and floating debris sent any number of boats to the bottom. River pirates posed an equally grave threat. One gang that worked the Ohio River invited passing crews to stop for a game of cards—and then cheated them out of their money. Another gang offered to pilot boats through a maze of tricky channels. Once in command, the "pilots" ran the boats aground and waiting gang members stole the cargoes. A third trick was to slip aboard at night and bore holes in a boat's hull. As the boat sank, the pirates sailed up in their skiffs and offered to help "save" the cargo. The luckless owners never saw their goods again.[10]

Like the Wilderness Road, the great days of the keelboat were numbered. In 1807, Robert Fulton's steamboat, the *Clermont*, amazed the world by making four miles an hour against wind and tide. Before long, shipbuilders at Pittsburgh and Frankfort were racing to build their own steamboats. "It will be a novel sight . . .," one writer observed, "to see a huge boat working her way up the windings of the Ohio, without the appearance of sail, oar, pole, or any manual labour about her."[11] A few months later the *Orleans* steamed down the river at the amazing speed of eight miles an hour.

A new age was dawning. The nation threw itself into the task of building new roads, laying railroad tracks, digging canals, and dredging river channels. In the rush to embrace the new, the old Wilderness Road was left behind.

★ THE TOLLGATE RAIDERS ★

The time was the early 1800s. Kentucky needed more and better roads, but no one wanted to pay the costs. Was there a cheap way to solve the problem? The state's lawmakers answered the question by awarding "turnpike rights" to local bidders. Once a contractor put in a road, the contractor was then free to collect tolls from anyone who wanted to use it.

The scheme seemed to pay off as the decades rolled by. Investors put up their money, built roads, and set up tollgates. In a nod to good works, pastors and funeral processions were given free passage. Freight wagons, coaches, horsemen, and farmers paid the going rate. A breeder driving pigs, sheep, goats, or cattle to market was charged one-quarter cent per head.[12] People grumbled that the roads were falling apart, but no one listened. Other complaints came from the backcountry, where traffic was too light to attract road-builders. Some communities were forced to build their own roads in order to move their goods to market.

In the decades after the Civil War, owners raised tolls and skimped on repairs. "It is up to us to take back our roads," Kentuckians told each other. In April 1897, a band of Anderson County riders forced the local toll collectors to tear down their gates. Raise the gates again, the riders warned, and we will be back with whips, tar, and feathers. News of the raid sparked copycat raids in other counties. When sheriffs did make arrests, friendly juries set their neighbors free.

A collector who fought back could expect rough treatment. One gatekeeper lost an eye in a scuffle. Another was held at gunpoint while masked riders burned down his house. Gatekeepers awoke to find that the Tollgate

Raiders had tacked notes to their homes. One note, its meaning clear despite the creative spelling, read:

NOTICE TO GATEKEEPER

We ast you not to collect no more tole, you must Not collect one cent if you do we are Going to Destroy your House with fire are Denamite. So you must Not collect No more tole at all. We don't want to do this but we want a Free Road are agoing to have it, if we have to kill and burn up everything. Collect no more tole we mean what we say, so Fair warning to you.[13]

In the end, the counties ended the toll war by buying the roads from their owners. Despite this victory, the roads decayed even further. Fearful of raising taxes, the state did not build a modern highway system until the rise of the automobile forced its hand. In 1912, lawmakers jumped on the bandwagon and voted to establish the Department of Good Roads.

THE WILDERNESS ROAD TODAY

Today much of the old Wilderness Road lies buried beneath farms, shopping malls, and playgrounds. The drivers who zip past the Cumberland Gap seldom notice that they are traveling one of the nation's historic routes. Asked about the westward movement, they are more likely to mention California than Kentucky.

The campers who stay in Cumberland Gap National Historical Park do not make that mistake. After they hike the trails and listen to rangers spinning tales of the Wilderness Road, the past comes to life. In the midnight hours Cherokee hunting parties slip through the woods. Next the long hunters stride by, flintlocks cocked and ready. Then, Daniel Boone's road-builders show up, followed by hordes of eager settlers. After a pause, armies of Civil War soldiers appear, their cannons carving deep ruts in the road. The tollgates go up a heartbeat later, raising tempers and slowing traffic. A final jump forward and modern road-builders return to lay smooth ribbons of asphalt. The traffic moves faster and faster. The past vanishes in a haze of dust and auto exhaust.

Hikers who venture into the backcountry find friendly mountain folk and hillsides untouched by modern strip mining and chainsaws. After a week's trek through the backcountry, Felix Gregory de Fontaine's word picture of his own journey along the Wilderness Road in 1870 makes more sense. The enjoyment, the journalist wrote, is in the "rocks and running streams, mountain-ferries, quaint old-fashioned mills, farm-houses and cabins perched like birds among the clefts of hills, . . . wild-flowers and waving grain."[1]

Restoring the Path of the Pioneers

One of the major events in the life of the Wilderness Road began early in the twentieth century. After years of neglect, builders began laying blacktop through the Cumberland Gap—the section whose treacherous twists and turns were known as the Devil's Stairway. Adding to the dangers of the corkscrew road, bandits often lay in wait near the switchbacks. Travelers armed themselves and sought company for the trip over the pass, as they had in the 1770s. The workmen finished blasting, scraping, and paving the new roadbed in 1908. A crowd cheered as wagons rolled smoothly over the blacktop on the day the road opened. When Henry Ford rolled out his first Model T's later that year, the Gap was ready for auto traffic. In a nation which counted only 680 miles of paved highway, the new road seemed like a minor miracle.[2]

The successful project led to further efforts to "get Kentucky out of the mud." The crown jewel in the improved road system opened in 1926. That was the year work crews opened the last stretch in the Dixie Highway (later renamed U.S. 25). After crossing the Cumberland Gap, northbound traffic now moved freely all the way to the Ohio River. Motels, cafés, and gas stations sprouted along the road. Although the growth was welcome, some people worried that urban sprawl was erasing the past. Lawmakers began looking for ways to save historic sites.

In 1943 Virginia, Kentucky, and Tennessee joined the crusade to save the Wilderness Road. Flashbulbs popped as the governors of the three states met to create the Cumberland National Park. Today support for preserving the Wilderness Road continues to gain steam. In 1996 the National Park Service finished construction of two 4,600-foot-long tunnels that allowed for the rerouting of U.S. 25E. With traffic switched to the tunnels, park officials "put back the Gap" by doing their best to restore the pass to the way it looked in the 1800s.

A Wilderness Road Itinerary

Does a visit to the Wilderness Road appeal to you? With much of the old road gone forever, you will have to trust guidebooks to help you find what is left. Here

This modern day caravan, its wagons hitched to teams of horses and mules, recalls life on the old Wilderness Road. The softly-sprung wagons and smooth roads provide these pioneers-for-a-day in Barboursville, Kentucky, with a far smoother ride than that enjoyed by their ancestors.

are some sites that deserve a visit (moving generally east to west):

Wilderness Road Regional Museum (Newbern, Virginia)

Housed in buildings that date back to the early 1800s, this museum helps keep the Wilderness Road alive. Adam Hance arrived here in 1810 and laid out twenty-eight lots along the Wilderness Road. Settlers who bought the lots agreed to build "a hewn log house at least one and a half stories high, with a shingled roof, brick or stone chimney, seams filled with lime mortar, [and] two glass windows with twelve lights [panes] each."[3] The Hance/Alexander family lived in the house built on Lot 2 until the 1970s. In addition to the buildings, the museum displays early period documents and photographs, artifacts from early Newbern, and household antiques.

Warrior's Path State Park (Kingsport, Tennessee)

This popular 950-acre family campground hugs the Holston River. The park takes its name from the Warrior's Path that once led Cherokee hunting parties across the mountains to Kentucky. The nine miles of trails that weave through the surrounding woodlands provide a taste of life on the ancient trail. After a brisk hike to Devil's Backbone and Holston Bluffs, visitors head back to the Patrick Henry Reservoir for swimming, fishing, and boating.

Cumberland Gap National Historical Park

Tourists who have time to hit only one Wilderness Road site should head for this twenty-thousand-acre wonderland. Located at the junction of Virginia, Tennessee, and Kentucky, the park is rich in history, culture, and natural resources. The visitor's center (just south of Middlesboro, Kentucky) uses exhibits and a short film to introduce the region's history. Another must-do exercise is the four-mile drive and short walk

Over the years, traffic over the Cumberland Gap increased dramatically—and so did the number of accidents. In time, travelers began referring to that steep and tricky stretch of road as "Massacre Mountain." Highway planners solved the problem by cutting a $265 million tunnel through Cumberland Mountain.

to Pinnacle Overlook (elevation 2,440 feet). From there it is easy to imagine how Thomas Walker felt when he first gazed into Kentucky back in 1750. Another thrill is to leave modern life behind as you hike along a segment of the old Wilderness Road. If you let your imagination run free, you might "see" a party of settlers striding along the road ahead of you.

A three-mile hike leads to 3,500-foot White Rocks and a breathtaking view into Virginia. In the late 1700s, the sight of the massive limestone outcropping told settlers they were nearing the Gap. A series of markers that tell the story of the heavy fighting that surged through the area in the 1860s fascinate Civil War buffs. Finally, for a glimpse of the old mountain lifestyle, visit Hensley Settlement atop Brush Mountain. The two Park Service farmers who live there demonstrate the farming methods that helped make mountain families self-sufficient.

Thomas Walker State Historic Site

This twelve-acre park lies five miles southwest of Barbourville on State Highway 459. The site features a replica of the cabin Thomas Walker built after crossing the Cumberland Gap in 1750. After a visit to the cabin, tourists can picnic, play minigolf, and (if their timing is good) hear a program of gospel music.

Daniel Boone National Forest

Once known as the Cumberland National Forest, this national treasure was renamed in 1966. The 670,000-acre park sprawls across eastern Kentucky's mountains and valleys. Much of the backcountry remains nearly as primitive as it was when Boone hunted there in the 1700s. Wild turkey and white-tailed deer are making a comeback. Grouse, foxes, ducks, quail, rabbits, mink, and raccoon are common. This national forest attracts fishermen, backpackers, kayakers, birdwatchers, and cross-country skiers. Hikers head for the Sheltowee Trace National Recreation Trail (Sheltowee means Big Turtle, the name given to Boone by the Shawnee). The

254-mile-long trail winds through deep canyons and swings past rock arches and natural bridges. Another popular feature is the Pioneer Weapons Hunting Area. This 7,480-acre tract near Cave Run Lake is reserved for hunters who use American Indian and pioneer weapons. Anyone who wants to bag a deer or a wild turkey must rely on a bow and arrow or a muzzle-loading rifle.

Fort Boonesborough and Boone Station

Fort Boonesborough lies a few miles southwest of Winchester on State Highway 627. Thanks to the

A low-lying cloud shrouds a Civil War gun emplacement and conjures up the ghosts of the soldiers who once stood guard here. This commanding position stands on Pinnacle Overlook in Cumberland Gap National Historic Park.

SOURCE DOCUMENT

WILDERNESS ROAD STATE PARK RENAMING CEREMONY
REMARKS OF JOHN PAUL WOODLEY, JR.
SECRETARY OF NATURAL RESOURCES, STATE OF VIRGINIA
DECEMBER 14, 1998

GENERALLY, WHEN WE TALK OF HALLOWED GROUND WE REFER TO OUR GREAT BATTLEFIELDS WHERE BRAVE MEN FOUGHT AND LOST THEIR LIVES TO PROTECT A WAY OF LIFE AND THEIR BELIEFS. THE WILDERNESS ROAD AND NEARBY CUMBERLAND GAP ARE HALLOWED GROUNDS FOR THOSE VERY SAME REASONS.

IT WAS THROUGH THIS AREA THAT GENERATIONS OF PIONEERS AND SETTLERS, BRAVE MEN, WOMEN AND CHILDREN WENT IN SEARCH OF A NEW LIFE. IN THEIR BATTLES TO CARVE OUT A NEW BEGINNING MANY LOST THEIR LIVES, BUT THEY ALL WERE INSTRUMENTAL IN BUILDING A COUNTRY WHERE WE STILL HOLD STRONG OUR BELIEFS. . . .

THIS NEW NAME REPRESENTS THE HISTORY OF THE REGION AND THE PARK'S VISION FOR THE FUTURE. THE MASTER PLAN DEVELOPED FOR THIS PARK, WITH SIGNIFICANT INPUT FROM THE PEOPLE OF THIS AREA, CALLS FOR THE FUTURE DEVELOPMENT OF A PIONEER VILLAGE AND OUTPOST. . . .

IN GOVERNMENT, AS IN LIFE, THERE ARE A FEW GREAT TRUTHS. IF YOU UNDERSTAND AND APPRECIATE THEM AND STRIVE TO LIVE BY THEM, YOU CANNOT GO FAR WRONG. ONE OF THOSE GREAT TRUTHS IS THAT VIRGINIANS LOVE OUR LAND, OUR WATERS, AND THE PURE AIR OF THIS GREAT COMMONWEALTH. THIS WAS TRUE WHEN DANIEL BOONE WALKED THESE GROUNDS, AND IT REMAINS TRUE TODAY.[5]

The Wilderness Road fell into disuse roughly 150 years ago. As this renaming ceremony shows, the famous old route has not been forgotten. Historic sites abound in the tristate area that the road once served. Tourists step back in time as they hike the Cumberland Gap, browse through regional museums, and wander through rebuilt frontier forts.

Kentucky Historical Society, the old fort has been rebuilt, and a trail guide leads visitors through the major events in Boonesborough's colorful history. After leaving the fort it is an easy drive to Boone Station. This state historic site marks the homestead where Boone settled after Boonesborough became too crowded for his liking. Boone's son Israel is buried in the cemetery there, along with his nephew Thomas. Both died in the Battle of Blue Licks in 1782.

Old Fort Harrod State Park

James Harrod's role in the settlement of Kentucky often is overlooked. This state park reminds visitors that Harrod established a fort here in July 1774—a year before Boone opened the Wilderness Road. From April to October, locals dressed in period costume demonstrate pioneer crafts. During the summer, actors perform in the amphitheater. *The Legend of Daniel Boone* introduces audiences to the famous woodsman and the early days of settlement in Kentucky. *Shadows in the Forest* tells the same story—from the viewpoint of the Shawnee.

★ GOING BACK IN TIME? ★
YOU MIGHT NEED A TRANSLATOR

Thanks to the British colonists who first settled this country, most Americans speak English as their native language. With that fact in mind, you might be tempted to guess that today's American English is much the same as that spoken yesterday.

To test that theory, let us travel back to the mid-1800s. Once you step out of your time machine, you will realize that language changes just as surely as do clothing styles. Here are a few of the colorful slang expressions (taken from period publications) that you might hear as you walk beside your great-great-great-grandparents. See how many of these 1800s expressions (printed in italics) you can interpret before you peek at the translations.[4]

Slang Expressions

1. David Johnson *acknowledged the corn*, and said that he was drunk.

2. *Jonathan* was hard to provoke; but when once you did get him up, he remained at a dead white heat for a long while.

3. We mistrust that the author of that statement saw a *Missouri toothpick*, and was frightened out of his wits.

4. "Who is that walking there with the *big bugs* in front?" he eagerly asked. "Why, don't you know? That is the Governor."

5. He declared he'd fight the whole *boodle* of 'em.

6. She is not very *chirk*, but more *chirkier* than she had been; and all our folks appear more

chirkier than they really feel, in order to *chirk* her up.

7. We should regard it as somewhat strange if we should require a *codfish aristocracy* to keep us in order.

8. Must all the world know all the *didoes* we cut up in the lodge room?

9. Stranger, if you don't shet your mouth a little closer than a Gulf clam, I'll *fix your flint* in short order.

10. Politicians don't care a *hooter*, so long as their own selfish ends are obtained.

Translations

1. *acknowledged the corn*—admitted the truth; confessed.

2. *Jonathan*—the American people; Uncle Sam.

3. *Missouri toothpick*—a long-bladed knife.

4. *big bugs*—bigwigs; important people.

5. *boodle*—a crowd of people.

6. *chirk*—cheerful.

7. *codfish aristocracy*—derisive term for people who have made a lot of money in business.

8. *didoes*—to cut up didoes was to get into mischief.

9. *fix your flint*—to settle a matter, by force if necessary.

10. *hooter*—a tiny amount.

★ TIMELINE ★

1646—Abraham Wood begins western movement by leading a party up the James River. By 1671 Virginians have reached the crest of the Blue Ridge Mountains.

1740s—Shawnee establish a trading town on ages-old Warrior's Path in Kentucky. Known as Es-kip-pa-kith-i-ka, the town dies within a few years.

1750—Dr. Thomas Walker finds an accessible route to Kentucky through the Cumberland Gap.

1763—American colonists rejoice as the French surrender their North American territories after the French and Indian War. The good feelings vanish when the Proclamation of 1763 closes the region west of the Appalachians to settlement.

1773—Daniel Boone leads a party of settlers through the Cumberland Gap. The party turns back after Shawnee raiders kill four of its members.

1774—James Harrod and his followers build Kentucky's first settlement and name it Harrodstown (later Harrodsburg).

1775—In March, Richard Henderson buys the territory between the Kentucky and Cumberland rivers from the Cherokee. During March and April, Daniel Boone and thirty axmen clear a route through the Cumberland Gap into Kentucky. The route later becomes known as the Wilderness Road.

1776—Americans fight the Revolutionary War and
-1781 win their independence.

1777—In the Year of the Bloody Sevens, savage fighting breaks out as the British and their American Indian allies nearly overrun American outposts in Kentucky.

1780—Battle of King's Mountain saves settlers from further attacks by British forces.

1783—Civilization begins to take hold in Kentucky. American Indian raids continue, but towns are growing as business and industry take root.

1784—John Filson's *Adventures of Colonel Daniel Boone, One of the Original Settlers of Kentucke* brings Daniel Boone, the Wilderness Road, and Kentucky to national attention.

1791—The Knoxville Road links the Wilderness Road with Knoxville, Tennessee, and opens more western lands to settlement.

1792—Kentucky joins the Union as the nation's fifteenth state. In the past ten years, seventy thousand people have entered Kentucky via the Wilderness Road.

1794—Battle of Fallen Timbers helps free Kentucky's settlers from the threat of attack by American Indian tribes that include the Shawnee, Miami, Chippewa, and Sauk.

1795—Kentucky legislature votes funds to widen the Wilderness Road so that it can carry wagon traffic.

1818—The National Road opens for traffic between Cumberland, Maryland and Wheeling, West Virginia. The new westward route reduces importance of the Wilderness Road.

1840s—Great days of the Wilderness Road have passed. Americans are pushing the frontier beyond the Mississippi along the Oregon, California, and Santa Fe Trails.

1861 -1865—The Wilderness Road serves as a key route for the movement of armies during the Civil War.

1908—Work crews open an all-weather highway across the Cumberland Gap.

1943—The governors of Virginia, Tennessee, and Kentucky dedicate the Cumberland National Historical Park to the pioneers who trekked west on the Wilderness Road.

1966—Visitors explore the newly renamed Daniel Boone National Forest. First established in 1937 as the Cumberland National Forest, the 670,000-acre preserve includes portions of the original Wilderness Road.

1998—Virginia dedicates the Wilderness Road State Park in Lee County to "generations of brave pioneers and settlers."

★ Chapter Notes ★

Chapter 1. The Land of Tomorrow

1. Robert L. Kincaid, *The Wilderness Road* (Indianapolis, Ind.: Bobbs-Merrill Co., 1947), p. 185.

2. H. Addington Bruce, *Daniel Boone and the Wilderness Road* (New York: Macmillan, 1951), pp. 298–299.

3. Steven A. Channing, *Kentucky: A Bicentennial History* (New York: W. W. Norton, 1977), p. 4.

4. William O. Steele, *The Old Wilderness Road: An American Journey* (New York: Harcourt, Brace & World, 1968), p. 23.

5. Ibid., pp. 28–29.

6. Kincaid, p. 47.

7. Frederick Jackson Turner, *The Significance of the Frontier in American History* (New York: Frederick Ungar Publishing Co., 1963), p. 35.

8. Steele, p. 55.

Chapter 2. War Comes to the Wilderness

1. Oliver La Farge, *A Pictorial History of the American Indian* (New York: Crown, 1957), pp. 20–22.

2. Steven A. Channing, *Kentucky: A Bicentennial History* (New York: W. W. Norton, 1977), pp. 23–24.

3. Thomas D. Clark, *Kentucky: Land of Contrast* (New York: Harper & Row, 1968), p. 4.

4. Ibid., p. 12.

5. Samuel Eliot Morison, *The Oxford History of the American People* (New York: Oxford University Press, 1965), p. 163.

6. Sanford Wexler, *Westward Expansion: An Eyewitness History* (New York: Facts on File, 1991), p. 305.

7. Robert L. Kincaid, *The Wilderness Road* (Indianapolis, Ind.: Bobbs-Merrill Co., 1947), p. 42.

8. William O. Steele, *The Old Wilderness Road: An American Journey* (New York: Harcourt, Brace & World, 1968), pp. 22–23, 34–37.

Chapter 3. "Every Heart Abounded with Joy"

1. William O. Steele, *The Old Wilderness Road: An American Journey* (New York: Harcourt, Brace & World, 1968), p. 61.

2. Ibid., pp. 61–62.

3. John Bakeless, *Daniel Boone* (Harrisburg, Pa.: Stackpole Co., 1939), p. 11.

4. Ibid., p. 5.

5. John Mack Faragher, *Daniel Boone: The Life and Legend of an American Pioneer* (New York: Henry Holt, 1992), p. 81.

6. Bakeless, p. 87.

7. Steven A. Channing, *Kentucky: A Bicentennial History* (New York: W. W. Norton, 1977), p. 21.

8. Reprinted in Robert Vexler, ed., *Chronology and Documentary Handbook of the State of Kentucky* (Dobbs Ferry, N.Y.: Oceana Publishers, 1978), pp. 111–113.

9. Bakeless, p. 395.

10. Steele, p. 122.

11. Faragher, p. 114.

12. Arthur Cuiterman, "Daniel Boone," *American Heritage Library Eagle Brigade*, n.d., <http://www.constitutional.net/042.html> (April 25, 2000).

Chapter 4. The Long, Hard Road

1. John Mack Faragher, *Daniel Boone: The Life and Legend of an American Pioneer* (New York: Henry Holt, 1992), p. 116.

2. Robert L. Kincaid, *The Wilderness Road* (Indianapolis, Ind.: Bobbs-Merrill, 1947), p. 104.

3. Faragher, pp. 132–137.

4. Ibid., p. 152.

5. William Allen Pusey, *The Wilderness Road to Kentucky; Its Location and Features* (New York: George H. Doran Company, 1921), p. 55.

6. Ibid., p. 114.

7. William O. Steele, *The Old Wilderness Road; an American Journey* (New York: Harcourt, Brace & World, 1968), p. 3.

8. H. Addington Bruce, *Daniel Boone and the Wilderness Road* (New York: Macmillan, 1951), p. 290.

9. Quoted in Steven A. Channing, *Kentucky: A Bicentennial History* (New York: W. W. Norton, 1977), p. 3.

10. Kincaid, pp. 171–172.

Chapter 5. A New Life Beyond the Mountains

1. John Bakeless, *Daniel Boone* (Harrisburg, Pa.: Stackpole, 1939), p. 313.

2. H. Addington Bruce, *Daniel Boone and the Wilderness Road* (New York: Macmillan, 1951), pp. 286–289.

3. Daniel Drake, *Pioneer Life in Kentucky, 1785–1800* (New York: Henry Schuman, 1948), p. 15.

4. Ibid., p. 27.

5. Theodore Roosevelt, *The Winning of the West*, Volume I (New York: The Review of Reviews, 1889), p. 131.

6. Drake, p. 25.

7. Bakeless, p. 104.

8. Drake, p. 53.

9. Ibid., p. 48.

10. Sanford Wexler, *Westward Expansion: An Eyewitness History* (New York: Facts on File, 1991), pp. 28–29.

11. Thomas D. Clark, *Kentucky: Land of Contrast* (New York: Harper & Row, 1968), p. 34.

12. Drake, p. 55.

13. Roosevelt, p. 140.

14. Ibid., p. 142.

15. Drake, p. 96.

16. Ibid., pp. 46–47.

17. Ibid., pp. 31–32.

Chapter 6. Kentucky Comes of Age

1. John Mack Faragher, *Daniel Boone: The Life and Legend of an American Pioneer* (New York: Henry Holt, 1992), p. 121.

2. Robert L. Kincaid, *The Wilderness Road* (Indianapolis, Ind.: Bobbs-Merrill Co., 1947), pp. 110–111.

3. Faragher, p. 239.

4. Steven A. Channing, *Kentucky: A Bicentennial History* (New York: W. W. Norton, 1977), p. 43.

5. Ibid., p. 73.

6. Daniel Drake, *Pioneer Life in Kentucky, 1785–1800* (New York: Henry Schuman, 1948), pp. 161–162.

7. Channing, p. 74.

8. Faragher, p. 307.

9. Quoted in H. Addington Bruce, *Daniel Boone and the Wilderness Road* (New York: The Macmillan Co., 1951), pp. 312, 315–317.

Chapter 7. End of an Era

1. Irene M. Franck and David M. Brownstone, *The American Way West* (New York: Facts on File, 1991), pp. 30–31.

2. Ibid., p. 115.

3. Quoted in H. Addington Bruce, *Daniel Boone and the Wilderness Road* (New York: Macmillan, 1951), p. 292.

4. Robert L. Kincaid, *The Wilderness Road* (Indianapolis, Ind.: Bobbs-Merrill, 1947), p. 189.

5. Ibid., p. 191.

6. Franck and Brownstone, p. 32.

7. Quoted in Franck and Brownstone, p. 34.

8. Sanford Wexler, *Westward Expansion: An Eyewitness History* (New York: Facts on File, 1991), p. 80.

9. Leland D. Baldwin, *The Keelboat Age on Western Waters* (Pittsburgh, Pa.: University of Pittsburgh Press, 1941), p. 181.

10. Ibid., pp. 117–118.

11. Ibid., p. 191.

12. Thomas D. Clark, *Kentucky: Land of Contrast* (New York: Harper & Row, 1968), p. 84.

13. Ibid., pp. 89–90.

Chapter 8. The Wilderness Road Today

1. Robert L. Kincaid, *The Wilderness Road* (Indianapolis, Ind.: Bobbs-Merrill, 1947), p. 288.

2. Ibid., pp. 350–352.

3. Staff, "The Wilderness Road Regional Museum," *WRRM*, 1998, <http://www.rootsweb.com/~vapulask/wrrm/about.htm> (April 25, 2000).

4. Marc McCutcheon, *The Writer's Guide to Everyday Life in the 1800s* (Cincinnati, Ohio: Writer's Digest Books, 1993), pp. 3–24.

5. *Wilderness Road State Park Renaming Ceremony*, n. d., <http://www.cns.state.va.us/snr/speeches/wilderness_road_renaming.htm> (May 1999).

★ Further Reading ★

Bakeless, John. *Daniel Boone*. Harrisburg, Pa.: Stackpole Co., 1965.

Bruce, H. Addington. *Daniel Boone and the Wilderness Road*. New York: The Macmillan Co., 1951.

Drake, Daniel. *Pioneer Life in Kentucky, 1785–1800*. New York: Henry Schuman, 1948.

Faragher, John Mack. *Daniel Boone: The Life and Legend of an American Pioneer*. New York: Henry Holt & Co., 1992.

Franck, Irene M. and David M. Brownstone. *The American Way West*. New York: Facts on File, 1991.

Kincaid, Robert L. *The Wilderness Road*. Indianapolis, Ind.: The Bobbs-Merrill Co., 1947.

Lawlor, Laurie. *Adventure on the Wilderness Road, 1775: American Sisters 4*. New York: Pocket Books, 1999.

Marvis, B. *Daniel Boone: Legends of the West*. Broomall, Pa.: Chelsea House Publishers, 1996.

McCarthy, Pat. *Daniel Boone: Frontier Legend*. Berkeley Heights, N.J.: Enslow Publishers, Inc., 2000.

Sanford, William R., and Carl R. Green. *Daniel Boone, Wilderness Pioneer*. Springfield, N.J.: Enslow Publishers, Inc., 1996.

Steele, William O. *The Old Wilderness Road: An American Journey*. New York: Harcourt, Brace & World, 1968.

Internet Addresses

Chinn, Col. George M. *Daniel Boone*. 1996. <http://americanwest.com/pages/boone.htm> (May 18, 2000).

Department of Conservation and Recreation. *Virginia State Parks: Wilderness Road State Park*. March 16, 2000. <http://www.state.va.us/~dcr/parks/wildroad.htm> (May 18, 2000).

Kentucky Historical Society. *Boone Station State Historic Site*. n.d. <http://www.kyhistory.org/agencies/parks/boonesta.htm> (June 1, 2000).

———. *Dr. Thomas Walker State Historic Site*. n.d. <http://www.kyhistory.org/agencies.parks/drwalker.htm> (June 1, 2000).

———. *Fort Boonesborough State Park*. n.d. <http://www.kyhistory.org/agencies/parks/ftboones.htm> (June 1, 2000).

National Park Service. *Cumberland Gap National Historic Park*. June 24, 1999. <http://www.nps.gov/cuga/index.htm> (May 18, 2000).

Staff. *Wilderness Road Regional Museum*. 1998. <http://www.rootsweb.com/~vapulask/wrrm/index.htm> (May 18, 2000).

★ INDEX ★